TESTIMONY OF A SEEKER

A young woman's journey to grace

JENNIFER JILL SCHWIRZER

Pacific Press® Publishing Association
Nampa, Idaho
Oshawa, Ontario, Canada

Edited by Jerry D. Thomas
Designed by Dennis Ferree
Cover photo by Christine Holmquist/Index Stock

The author assumes full responsibility for the accuracy of all facts and quotations as cited in this book.

Printed in the United States of America

Schwirzer, Jennifer Jill, 1957-
Testimony of a Seeker : a young woman's journey to grace / Jennifer Jill Schwirzer.
p. cm.
ISBN 0-8163-1769-0 (paper)
1. Schwirzer, Jennifer Jill, 1957- 2. Christian biography—United States. I. Title.
BR1725.S396 A3 2000
286.7'092—dc21
[B]

99-049009

00 01 02 03 04 • 5 4 3 2 1

Contents

Preface

I first became acquainted with Jennifer Jill Schwirzer when she came to our church to perform concerts. Although Vermont is not lacking in the fine arts it isn't often that we are treated to Seventh-day Adventist musicians. I don't think I've ever missed one of her concerts and they have always been a great blessing to me. Over the years I have collected many of her CDs and tapes.

But, I didn't really get to know Jennifer until a retreat my husband and I went on several years ago during a troubled time in our marriage. She was giving a seminar entitled Healing Inner Wounds: Biblical Recovery. I'm not sure why she remembered me, but she did and we talked for awhile. Jennifer is one of those people you instinctively trust. A lot of things in our lives are similar and I felt as though we bonded during the weekend.

When I read the manuscript for *Testimony of a Seeker,* I realized how very much we do have in common. Although my life has not been nearly as exciting as Jennifer's, I faced a lot of the same problems. Her complete honesty about topics I would shy away from confronting helped me to face them in my own life.

I have often thought that our churches would be more effective as safe haven for broken people rather than showcases for the perfect. Sadly, confronted by the dazzling display of perfection the hurting are too afraid to admit it and hide their pain. I am one of those people. Maybe you are too. In this book you will meet someone who was also hurting and confused and alone. She found the only real solution to any of our heartaches in Jesus.

He is the only answer, the only solution, to all the needs of our heart. *He is available to us every minute; we can go to Him for whatever we need: peace, comfort, love, healing.* He has an endless supply. Every need of our heart can be filled because of Jesus' gift of love to us and all that we seek we shall find.

In Jennifer's story I hope you can find the courage to confront your own problems, whatever they may be, with honesty and strength knowing that you are not alone. We're all human and we're all hurting in one way or another. None of us is as perfect as we pretend to be. It's time to be real with each other and admit it. It's only then that we have anything tangible to offer the hurting people who surround us.

Céleste perrino Walker

Introduction

When Pacific Press® asked me to write my story, I thought, "But I don't *have* a story. I was never a prostitute, drug dealer or politician. What do I have to say?"

As you can see by the book you are at this moment holding in your hands, I did have something to say after all. Hopefully it will be of a character that will uplift and help you in your own journey.

But some of what I relate may not seem to be so on the surface. It's not all positive. I talk about my experiences in a straightforward way, at the same time making an effort not to bring the mind of the reader down to a low level. Eating disorders, fanaticism, the blood and guts of faulty human relationships, dishonesty, sexual abuse and harassment all have a place on these pages, along with some other "bummers" I have been through. But I tried, oh, I tried, to relate the truth while sparing you the unnecessary details. I tried to bring positive lessons out of negative experiences. I tried to show that "all things work together for good to them that love God" (Romans 8:28, KJV).

On the positive side, the never-ending love and care of God, the blossoming of pure romance, and the beauty of truth as it unfolded before my mind and other happy moments are here too, hopefully making your reading experience one of more pleasure than pain.

I have used pseudonyms for the majority of people. As the expression goes, "the names have been changed to protect the innocent." More accurately, "the names have been changed to protect the guilty." Yes, I even sought to protect the guilty as much as I could without failing to relate information that was vital to the story. My intention was not to expose or villianize, it was to share the lessons I learned that others might benefit from them. I would ask that if you relate the contents of this book to others, that you do it in the same spirit. Ask yourself, as I did, "Why am I talking about this? What did I learn from it?"

While all the events of this story are true, there were some liberties taken in the reconstruction of the chronology of the events. I also added short vignettes in the beginning of each chapter that are a mixture of fact and fiction. Of course I don't know what happened in the angelic realm of my life, but I can imagine. And imagine I did.

So please read, and ask others to read. My prayer is that my story will inspire you to take your own story seriously, tracing the hand of God in the events of your life as I have in mine. These simple stories we share are a distinguishing mark of God's people (see Revelation 12:17). As heaven condescended in Jesus Christ, it condescends to fill each of our lives, making it not just another life, but a *testimony*. May my testimony inspire you to share your own with whoever God leads across your path.

❦ ❦ ❦ ❦

Leave the wounds alone and let them heal
Let your heart believe what you can't feel
All of this defeat will be swept away
Sooner than you think, you will want to say,

"The language of shame is no more on my tongue
I've forgotten the words and the song can't be sung
And I will not be captive to the ghosts of the past
They may come here to haunt me, but I know it won't last
I don't care about me, but I know Someone does
And He said it with blood in the language of love."

From the song "The Language of Love" on the CD *Banish the Myth.* Copyright 1995, Jennifer Jill Schwirzer.

❦ ❦ ❦ ❦

CHAPTER 1

Little Martyr

Spring, 1968.

Afternoon recess at Bayside Elementary School, an upper-middle-class suburb of Milwaukee, Wisconsin. Some of the hundred or so playground occupants are doing what one would expect, jumping rope, playing tetherball, shooting baskets. But there are others gathered off to the side of the building. They are circling around a golden-haired adolescent girl wearing a bright green and blue sweater dress. She looks calm, but one can see the sweat of panic on her upper lip.

"But why?" she says, looking imploringly at the crowd.

"Because you're a boyfriend stealer!" shouts a lanky girl in a short, tight skirt, apparently the ringleader of the group. Taking a step closer, she cuts loose with a string of profanity and shoves the golden-haired girl to the ground. The girl offers little resistance, almost as if she accepts the unfair sentence this young judge has passed upon her. Crashing backwards, she feels long arms pin her shoulders to the ground.

"Yeah!" several voices in the crowd cry out, "you're such a slut!" The crowd circles closer to her like wolves closing in upon their prey.

❦❦❦❦

I will begin my story at the point when life lost its simplicity—those pimple-ridden teenage years I would in some ways rather forget. Oh, there were redeeming elements, such as music, to take the edge off of life's harsh realities. I have always wanted to be a songwriter. As a teenager, I idolized Joni Mitchell, the poet-muse of the flower child generation. Her ballads were set to acoustic guitar with the likes of James Taylor crooning in the background. I could sit in my room for hours whining along to "Blue" and "The Last Time I Saw Richard." Then my older brother would come to my door and impersonate me, after which I would sit in silence and wish I could write a song. Oh, how I wanted to be a songwriter.

The fact was, I did not know what to say. I had no burning interest in politics and I was too embarrassed to write a love song. So I learned *her* songs, plucking my guitar and singing softly for friends. I went on to learn a Neil Young song about the National Guard killing four teenage protesters at Ohio State University. "Ohio" even made me famous with a few people! "For a freak you're a good kid," one fan wrote in my yearbook, "you got a nice voice and you play a mean guitar." Little comments like that set off sparks in my soul. I wanted more than anything to express myself—whatever myself was—in music and words.

I have learned since those days that I often admire people who do things that I will eventually learn to do. I was awed by Joni Mitchell's gift partly because I had the same gift, although it was buried within me. Between those awkward teenage years and now, my gift has been cut loose, giving birth to hundreds of songs. Maybe even a thousand. And there was a time when I couldn't write so much as one.

But this story is bigger than the saga of a songwriter. More than just liberating my poetic gift, the Lord God has freed my soul. He has made something beautiful out of my life. In this respect my story is the story of every person's potential in Christ. If God can take a bewildered teenager like I was and bring a song out of her, He can do anything. And that means He can do anything with you. I have no hopes of impressing you with my being exceptional; I am not. The encouragement you receive from this journal will not be from a great person, but from a great God working through an average person.

❦ ❦ ❦ ❦

I was born into a picture-perfect, White-Anglo-Saxon-Protestant family. There was a beautiful lady who married a strong man. The man got a good job and they settled into a pretty house. Then the children came; a boy, then a girl, then another boy, and then another girl. They were all healthy and cute. The beautiful lady stayed home with the children and the strong man went off to work every day. The snapshots of those years are like pages out of a Norman Rockwell portfolio—sparkly Christmases and vacations to Florida, laughing faces around a brimming table. Life was idyllic, and I was a simple, content child.

Then reality hit.

We had moved from a small town in Ohio to a suburb of Milwaukee, Wisconsin—a much more cosmopolitan area. There I experienced ridicule and rejection for the first time in my life. My first day at the new school, I wore little white ankle socks, and found most of the other girls had graduated to nylons and mini skirts. In the sometimes cruel mind of an adolescent, deviating from the norm of fashion is a crime worthy of public humiliation. I was ignored, teased, and taunted. I went home after school and cried every day. My mom tried to get me to befriend girls who were like me—unpopular—but I could not rest until the "brat pack" allowed me admittance. Something within me blazed ahead even when I knew the territory was not safe because I wanted to run with the fast horses.

Finally I gained a measure of acceptance, but it was always tenuous and it wasn't long before a strange phenomenon began to take place. The group would pick a person they wanted to hurt, and they would turn upon them like sharks in a feeding frenzy. From the moment this poor individual entered the school doors until they boarded the bus to go home, they suffered a continual stream of ridicule and abuse. I watched for the most part when this occurred, too tenderhearted to join in the abuse, but too cowardly to stick up for the person. Then one day it was my turn.

Many long weeks passed during which my "friends" harassed me hour by hour, in the classroom, on the playground, in the halls. There was no specific infraction I was guilty of, just a general malice that decided I was next. Just when I thought the malicious treatment would end, it got far, far worse than I ever thought it could.

On a sunlit playground, at an age when we all should still have been playing hopscotch, these "friends" formed a plan to repay me for a crime I never committed. Under the pretense that I had tried to steal another girl's boyfriend (I never even spoke to him!), they pinned me to the ground and viciously molested me. As a crowd of kids watched, I was a little martyr without a cause. The worst fear of any person—public ridicule and abuse—was heaped upon me at an age when that very fear is at its most acute. It was an adolescent's nightmare, a young lifetime of terrors fulfilled in one twenty-minute recess.

Our teacher, Mrs. Manns, saw my mud-streaked clothes and disheveled hair as I sat trying to recover from the ordeal. "I know who did this, and it's just horrible!" she yelled at my abusers. She couldn't punish them, though, because she knew it would bring on even more resentment of me, and possibly more torture.

So many of our lives are littered with instances of suffering at the hands of our fellow creatures. Strangers, relatives, friends, line up in memory's hall of infamy, weapons of sexual and physical mischief in their hands. Why is it so, when we were created for harmony? It must be that sin has caused "most people's love to grow cold" (Matthew 24:12, NAS).

But for those of us who have those bitter memories, I can say without hesitation that God can use it all. I know how this has worked for me. Because of that day, when a mocking crowd surrounded me, I can imagine better how Jesus felt when He said, "many bulls have surrounded me . . . they open wide their mouth" (Psalm 22:12,13, NAS). Because I have been humiliated before jeering onlookers, I appreciate more the fact that Jesus, "endured the cross, despising the shame" (Hebrews 12:2, NAS).

Our mind's eye has largely accepted the rendition of the cross that masterpiece paintings have given us. Beautiful as they may be, they are not accurate. Jesus hung *naked* before the people whom He died to clothe with His righteousness. During His trial He "received every indignity." "Never was criminal treated in so inhuman a manner as was the Son of God" (*Desire of Ages,* 710). Every species of abuse was heaped upon our Jesus. Certainly His wounded side holds a refuge for those of us who are victims of the same.

There is hope and light in this for the walking wounded, because "of all the gifts that Heaven can bestow upon men, fellowship with Christ in His sufferings is the most weighty trust and the highest honor" (*The Desire of Ages,* 225). My own small sufferings have brought me into fellowship with the crucified Christ. I can't imagine a better resolution to the painful dilemma of abuse.

❦ ❦ ❦ ❦

Eventually, we all became more civilized. I found a friend or two, and became the captain of the cheerleading team. I had the distinctive honor of being the first girl in fourth grade to go steady with a boy. I had earned the respect of my peers, and I was happy for it.

And this served to replace what I really needed, which was God's acceptance. I had no knowledge of God except what I heard at church, which basically went in one ear and out the other. The kind of church I attended advocated the "social gospel" but didn't focus much on personal salvation. No one ever approached me in regards to my own relationship with God or shared a personal Savior with me. The youth leader was fond of New Age ideas, and once read my aura, but never talked to me about Christ. The pastor, a charismatic man who was greatly admired by his congregation, divorced eventually, and the choir director left his wife to marry the lead soprano. All of this touched my idealistic young heart like pins to a balloon. Cynicism began to take root as I saw the faults of professed Christians, and I came to the conclusion that Christianity was just a culture and the church a country club.

My parents had high ideals. My dad was a hard-working, honest, faithful businessman. My mom trained as a speech pathologist and always encouraged me to do good and help people less fortunate than myself. They tried their best to keep me on the "straight and narrow," but I don't think they realized how much the world had changed since they were young. For me to live by their standards in the social circles I ran in was like asking me to swim up Niagra Falls. I was a very curious kid, and one that wanted to try everything every other kid tried. So during those pre-high school years, I ran as wild as I could run and not get caught. Then one day God looked down upon me from heaven and said, "She needs a wake-up call."

❦❦❦❦

I want to forgive before they are sorry
Like You forgave when I had no clue
Tell me, how can I be bitter and angry
When I keep fresh in mind what I did to you?

From the song "In Christ Medley" on the CD *Chance of Rain.* Copyright 1998, Jennifer Jill Schwirzer.

❦❦❦❦

CHAPTER 2

The Fire

Winter, 1970.

A well-manicured brick home in Fox Point, Wisconsin is empty, except for a company of sinister creatures both unseen and unheard, standing outside the living room window. A curl of smoke seeps through the screen, the sight of which provokes a certain wicked cheering among the dark beings. Before long, smoke is billowing out of every downstairs window. The evil angels begin to dance.

One year later, two worried adolescent girls sit in a sparsely furnished sunroom, twirling their thumbs and glancing at each other. Wordless memories shoot between them almost telepathically . . . a siren, a mob of neighbors, a picture window pouring out flames. "Don't tell anyone!" the taller had hissed under her breath, as the other gave a tense nod. Now they sit in silence, like two wild but caged animals, hoping for mercy, expecting none. A tall, dark-haired man appears in the doorway. Doomsday has arrived.

❦❦❦❦

I believe that people are like chemicals. Certain ones react with certain others . That's how it was with Sue Cook, a funny, artistic girl who lived in the same suburb I did. There was tremendous chemistry in our relationship. We enjoyed many hours of silliness and adventure together, never at a loss for things to do because both of us were creative and supercharged with the electricity of youth. But like any two unprincipled young girls left to their own devices, we did stupid things. We went through a phase of hyperventilating until we fainted, which we did for "fun" until one girl passed out in the bathroom at school and hit her head on a toilet seat, resulting in a concussion! Not learning from that, we went on to smoking cigarettes. The ironic thing about this was that I was the one who talked my mom into quitting only years before. I knew I was a hypocrite, but the lure of amusement was too great for me. Unused to nicotine, we would receive a momentary "buzz," and giggle until it wore off.

One day we were busy smoking at Sue's house, and suddenly we heard the door slam. Thinking we would be caught, we ran to see who it was, finding that it was only the dog. When we returned to the couch, we found that I had dropped the lit cigarette between the cushions. It had burned into the box springs and could not be retrieved. We poured water on it, shrugged, and sprayed some air freshener. Sue went out somewhere, and I went home.

I was in my room getting ready for bed that evening when my kid brother burst through the door. The moments that followed are frozen in my mind. Scott's twirpy little chest was expanded with excitement and his eyes were wide brown alarm clocks. He then yelled seven words I will never forget, "Jennifer, Sue Cook's house is BURNING DOWN!"

I rode my bike, I ran, I *flew* to Sue's house. Sure enough, a mob gathered. As I ran, I stumbled upon Jim Rice, a short, thin classmate of mine with coke-bottle glasses.

"Jim, this is all my fault!" I spilled, "We were smoking and I dropped a burning cigarette into the couch! I know that's what happened!" Jim stared speechlessly through the glasses while I tore ahead to the house. I didn't realize he was the last person I would confess the matter to for a long time.

As I drew near, I could see that the inside of the house was black. The sickening blackness of charred memories kept from devouring everything only by the fact that the house was brick. Out of sheer guilt I made a vow to myself. I vowed that I would grow up, get a job and repay the family for all the damage I had caused. I was willing to confess, to take the blame, suffer the penalty, anything but to feel the shame of what I had done.

When I found Sue, our eyes locked in mutual knowing, but she was afraid to let the truth come out. "Don't tell anyone!" she hissed. I was absolutely torn. How could I carry this burden of guilt, but how could I defy my best friend?

❦ ❦ ❦ ❦

The next week, Sue and I snuck out of school and walked to her house during the lunch break. We wandered from room to charred room, inspecting the carbon-coated remains of her childhood. We did not cry at first. We *laughed* at the melted record albums and singed clothes. We were too young to even comprehend the ordeal, so we *laughed* . . . until we got to her piano. There, on what remained of a beautiful instrument, was a piece of music Sue had been learning, charred around the corners, but not so burned that we could not read the song title, "Fire and Rain," by James Taylor. Then we cried.

The hush plan worked for about a year. Sue moved to another town, but we stayed in close touch, corresponding by phone and letters. But eventually one of the letters which referred to the cause of the fire was found by Mr. Cook, and a meeting was called.

Now, Mr. Cook had never seemed to me to be a very affable fellow. He was, of all things, a lawyer, and a very reserved, professional man. I had never seen his light side, and I assumed that he didn't have one. I did not look forward to discussing with him the fact that I had incinerated his house. Nevertheless, one Saturday morning I found myself sitting in his sunroom with Sue and that very item on the agenda. The whole affair was quite perfunctory. There were no smiles, no tears, just a short talk and the pronouncement of the sentence: I had to tell mom.

Needless to say, mom was not happy. I can still see her face while we sat in the family station wagon, parked at the local shopping center.

"Mom, there's something I need to tell you," I said in a wimpy voice.

"What?" Her beautiful black eyes had the classic "oh, no" look that any mother's would have after hearing those words.

"Uh . . . do you remember the Cook's fire? Well . . . I was responsible for it."

Mom crumbled right there in front of me and it broke my heart. I couldn't have devised a more torturous punishment for myself if I had been a member of the KGB.

Life went on after that, but I was never quite so carefree as I was before the fire. I now knew what serious guilt felt like, and I didn't like it. I had learned that doing wrong had consequences. I wish I could say that I had learned my lesson, but it's not the consequence of sin that turns a person away from sin, it's the Lord. And I didn't know Him . . . yet.

❦ ❦ ❦ ❦

Decades after the fire, my mother was still friends with Mr. Cook. She called me one holiday season and said that he wanted to buy two of my CDs for his daughters for Christmas. "Just send them with a bill," mom said. I remembered the fire and my vow to repay the Cooks for the loss of their house. Being older and wiser, I knew that the house had been covered by insurance, and that he didn't hold me accountable for what I did as a teenager. Still, I was not about to send Mr. Cook a bill, knowing how much I "owed" him. I wrote him a note that I sent with the CDs. The note read, "Mr. Cook, please take these CDs free of charge. Consider this a down payment on the great debt that I owe you."

He wrote me back, and his words meant more to me than he knew. In fact, they have come to illustrate the reality of the gospel. He said, "I never considered, even for a moment, that you owed me anything."

In my youthful ignorance I had vowed to pay a debt I could never pay. I didn't realize two things; one, just how great the debt was, and two, just how forgiving Mr. Cook was. In the same way we so often vow to pay God back, not realizing the enormity of the debt, nor how forgiving the Lord is. This idea that we can repay God is called *legalism*.

Legalism, or being "under the law" is a disease that we all suffer from. We are by nature prone to want to atone for our own guilt through some kind of works program. From this basic tendency has sprung a smorgasbord of world religions that are all based on the same basic idea of salvation by works. But far from actually doing what it purports to, legalism separates us from God. The Bible tells us why in Ephesians 2:8, 9:

> "For by grace you have been saved through faith; and that not of yourselves, *it is* the gift of God; not as the result of works, that no one should boast."

If God did allow us to save ourselves by our works, we would "boast," meaning that we would become proud. Pride makes an idol of self and separates the soul from the Savior. So a "works trip" actually leads people to hell instead of heaven. Not a very good deal, is it?

A much better deal is really not a deal at all. It's a gift. It's the gift of God to every lonely youth, every stressed father, every overworked mom. It's the gift of God in His Son Jesus Christ, living and dying for you. Believing in that Gift leads to salvation by grace. The ultimate product of that faith experience is an obedient life, but in that life good works are a fruit of salvation and not a means of it.

Do you appreciate God's gift? You will if you really comprehend it. True faith is not just a mental assent to the truth. Devils have that kind of faith, for, "the demons also believe, and shudder" (James 2:19, NAS). True faith includes appreciation and gratitude. Mary was filled with gratitude, and it led her to anoint Jesus with precious ointment that cost her a year's wages. He said to her, "Your faith has saved you; go in peace" (Luke 7:50, NAS). If we really believe, our hearts will be softened. We will be led to love and forgive people as Jesus has loved and forgiven us.

If you're like me, you find at times that the hard knocks of life put calluses on your heart. You begin to harbor anger. Your spirit becomes jaded. All of this comes from forgetting the great debt we owe Jesus. To recognize His mercy is to be filled with it. Take time today to hear the good news all over again. Let the Spirit point to the sacrifice of Jesus and say to you, "I never considered, even for a moment, that you owed me anything."

❦❦❦❦

But there's a love that differs from any other kind
That towers over every love that you or I could find
Go, search the world over now
But I have searched enough
And none has ever come close to
God's agape love

From the song "God's Agape Love" on the CD *Songs in the Night.* Copyright 1989, Jennifer Jill Schwirzer.

❦❦❦❦

CHAPTER 3

Infatuation

Spring, 1972.

In a sea of blue jeans and flannel shirts a girl sat, her wavy gold hair spilling over a book. Loud groups of students, none of which she belonged to, created a bedlam of noise. Raising her head to rub her neck, she spotted a dark-haired boy across the hall, walking hand-in-hand with a girl she had known since grade school. Rick Kagen and Jerry Joslove, she thought. I never would have put them together. He is so cool, and she's so shallow. Oh well, I guess I just have to get used to being left out.

Being freshmen, these teenagers had come from different elementary schools and met in the new social vista of Nicolet High. Young love affairs sprang up everywhere the young girl looked, but for her there was only schoolbooks and her deep, lonely thoughts.

At the same moment, an interview took place in heaven between a being of majestic bearing and a beautiful angel. The majestic one spoke with gentle power.

"We have determined that this earthling is the kind that will do whatever she does with all her heart. Unfortunately, that means evil as well as good. Her earthly father has said she does things the hard way. And he is right. We perceive, however, that after suffering some of the effects of her course of sin, she may turn from it in search of something better. Look at her. She is lonely. But still, she does not receive God, though His Spirit pursues her. We have received word that a certain young man

named Rick will come into her life. Because this relationship may ultimately teach her that true love comes only from God Himself, we have decided to grant permission."

❦❦❦❦

Sue moved to Phoenix, and I was left to face high school without a close friend. For the better part of my freshman year I wandered the halls alone, unable to find my niche among the twenty-five hundred students. For the most part I kept to myself, but I did have one friend named Jim who I talked with on the bus to and from school. Our common ground was that we were both totally engrossed in the books of J. R. R. Tolkien, which are tales of hobbits, elves and fairies. These books became my escape from a less than cheerful existence.

There were three basic cliques at Nicolet High School; the freaks, the greasers, and the jocks. The "freaks" were the Jerry Garcia wannabees with long hair and faded jeans. They did plenty of drugs and rebelled against "the establishment." The "greasers" got their name from the Brill Cream they used to keep their hair slicked back. They tore around in hot rod cars with their heavily made-up girlfriends, and enjoyed drinking. The "jocks" did everything all the other kids did, but they hid it better, preserving a clean-cut American image and participating in sports and for the girls, cheerleading.

I was faced with a real dilemma that year. I needed a social life, but I didn't really fit in anywhere. Cheerleading lost its appeal when I saw the plastic personalities of the girls that carried the pom-poms. I was no greaser, and the freak's obsession with drugs bothered me. There were kids that didn't belong to any clique, and I sort of floated among them for a time . . . and then there was Rick. Rick put me on the map.

He was one of the "Prince Charmings" of the freshman class with long black hair, eyes as green as a summer lawn, and usually some pretty girl beside him. Rick went through bags of marijuana and girlfriends at roughly the same rate—a new one every week or so. When I met him on a ski trip, I was surprised at how friendly and personable he was, rather than being stuck up as I would have assumed. How nice, I thought, that he's willing to be cordial to me, a nobody! We actually skied together most of one day and talked on the bus ride home. I had a nice time with him, but I knew it was going to be back to school the next day, and our communication would end. He would be off with his popular friends, and I would be back to my hobbit books.

I was not in the habit of praying, but algebra class was a good place to start. It was boring enough to bring anyone to their knees, especially a lonely teenage girl with a bad case of infatuation. As I sat there that Monday, I thought over the events of the weekend and I decided that I should hope for the impossible. "Dear God," I prayed silently, "I have never really asked you for anything . . . but could you do this one thing for me? I want Rick to like me . . . I want to be his girlfriend . . . so just this one thing, God, and then I will leave you alone."

While the teacher droned on about the power of three squared, I made a little origami bird out of my math assignment. It was as tiny as I felt in that overcrowded high school, but delicate and exquisite, and more worthy of notice than the big paper airplanes flying around the room. When the bell rang, I walked down the hall toward the place where the freaks congregated between classes. There was Rick, his never failing smile flashing white teeth at whoever was lucky enough to see them. I crept up with my little bird, not feeling much bigger myself, and in one bracing act of courage I placed it in his upturned hand and walked away.

Little did I know that my feelings for Rick were mutual all along. Not much time passed before we were an item, seen more often together than apart. Suddenly I was an honorary member of Rick's high-society clique, and all his pretty ex-girlfriends, who had ignored me up to that point, were looking me up and down and wondering what I had that they didn't. Actually I wondered myself, but eventually I settled into the fact that, believe it or not, he really did like me. A mutual obsession set in. Rick was the centerpiece of my life and I was his, and most other interests were laid aside.

There were good things about our relationship. We both had ten-speed bikes that we rode to and from school, and most afternoons we would ride to one of the parks in the city and enjoy the beauty of nature. Even though Rick loved to get high on drugs of various kinds, we never got high together, as we enjoyed each other's company enough not to feel the need for a diversion. We both had a spite for Western materialism and would often talk of what we would do when we were old enough to leave home. The dream was to move "back to the land" living in a remote area in a log cabin, growing our own food and dressing in animal skins. We shared high ideals, even if they were a little extreme.

But there were problems. Rick's parents were not very happy with his relationship with me because they were Jewish and were mortified by the possibility of his marrying a Gentile. This made me all the more attractive to him I think, him being in a rather rebellious stage of life. Likewise, my parents were suspicious of Rick with his long hair and renegade friends. One night Rick and I got picked up by the police for trespassing in the bird sanctuary—something we found rather funny because it was really such an innocent thing for us to get in trouble for. My dad didn't think it was funny, though, and let me know in no uncertain terms after he picked me up at the police station. Dad's rage did not help matters. It only drove me further away from my parents and deeper into the refuge of my friends. There I felt accepted, especially in the arms of this boy-wonder who could take away all my pain with a smile.

❦ ❦ ❦ ❦

As much as it sounds like a fairy tale come true, this teenage romance was harmful to me in the long run. If I could go back in time now and sit myself down, I would say what I say to so many young lovers now, "It's just too much, too soon, and too young!"

Reckless romance can program a person for failure in future relationships because it teaches us to view love as a feeling. Part of the reason we believe this is because we use the same word for all types of love. We read "God is love" in the Bible and then hear, "Baby, you give good love" on the radio. Since our language does not differentiate between love and lust, often our minds don't.

The Greek language has several words for love. *Eros* is the word used to describe romantic or sexual love and *agape* is used to describe God's unconditional love. Most of us at some point lose sight of God's agape love, and when we do, a counterfeit is quick to present itself. Love's most clever imposter is *eros*. The media bombards us with the message that sexual infatuation is true love.

A little background on the origin of the word *eros* helps us see how wrong universal ideas of love are. Eros, was the name of a god of Greek mythology. He was reincarnated in Roman mythology as Cupid whom we know of through Valentine's Day. If Cupid shot someone with his arrow, it was thought, there was no way to escape "loving" the person he wanted you to love. According to that legend, love is an overpowering force—a feeling that can't be resisted.

But the Bible presents a different picture of love. According to this picture, love is a matter of choice. God invites us to respond to His love, and though He presents strong incentives, He does not coerce. "Open to me," He says to His bride, "my sister, my darling, ... my perfect one!" (Song of Solomon 5:2, NAS). " 'Behold, I stand at the door and knock;' " He invites us, " 'if anyone hears My voice, I will come in to him, and will dine with him, and he with Me' " (Revelation 3:20, NAS).

Our capacity for *eros* love is a powerful force that, like fire, can bring life when contained and death when not contained. So many look back at their lives and wish that they had allowed the fire of their natural affections to be channeled by God for good. The good news to those of us who have lost at love is that God will give us "beauty for ashes" (Isaiah 61:3, KJV). The ashes are a result of the poor choices we have made, but God gives repentance as a gift to those who are willing to receive it. Through this gift, even ashes can be made beautiful, for the ashes turned us to the Lord.

1 Corinthians 13, "the Love Chapter," has nine descriptions of love in the negative and only seven in the positive. This means that God uses negative phrases like, "love is *not* rude" and "love does *not* envy" as much as He uses affirmative statements like "love *is* patient" and "love *is* kind." God knows where we are coming from. He can use even our past mistakes if we allow Him to show us love of another kind.

❦❦❦❦

One pair of arms that are always open
One pair of always loving eyes
One thing you know when your heart is broken
There's a place for you waiting in Christ

❦❦❦❦

CHAPTER 4

Golden Light

Winter, 1973.

In a small living room in downtown Milwaukee a group of people in street clothes sat with several individuals wearing white robes and turbans. A man, obviously the leader of the group, spoke while a devotee offered the people cups of tea. No one interrupted as the leader droned on, his large blue eyes occasionally rolling back into his head. "You have to come in contact with the energy force within you . . . the part of you that is connected with the universe. In order to do that, you must push yourself beyond your limits. If you don't work out your karma in this life, you will have to work it out in the next. There is no short cut. Only those who devote their lives to finding it will reach enlightenment. Nothing is free. You have to work."

Unseen to the attendants in the room were the dark angels who sat and squatted around the room. They seemed in such sharp contrast to the appearance of holiness made by the people wearing white robes and turbans. But in fact, there was an unconscious collusion between the two groups. Unconscious, that was, on the part of the people. For the devils it was a conscious endeavor if there ever was one.

"This is what we do best!" said one of the dark beings through black lips. "Bind people in cords of legalism. Teach them that they can save themselves. Make them regard the religion of the One we hate seem like a crutch and an escape. This way, we can make them wholly evil even while they think they are becoming good."

❦❦❦❦

Rick's friends didn't like me. One of the main reasons was that I persuaded Rick to stop taking psychedelic drugs, which he and his buddies had made a weekly ritual. In fact, these fellows could not seem to find anything more interesting than getting high. At parties they would sit around with Grateful Dead music blaring and play air guitar, grinning stupidly at each other, stoned out of their minds.

Meanwhile, I began to feel a longing for something other than what the weekend parties had to offer. I started to meet people, read books, and ask questions about life that most kids would never dream of. I became quite philosophical and analytical, and earned the nickname "the shrink." One of the first things I began to analyze was the American way of life. We were materialistic, wasteful, and destructive to the environment as far as I was concerned. We ate processed foods and dead animals, and I believed that there was something wrong with that picture.

Soon I met a vegetarian named Morgan who was dating a friend of mine. He was a wiry fellow with long, frizzy hair and a beard, which he stroked like a wise old sage as he made profound statements. "If I had to eat rats, I'd eat rats!" he said. "But there are better options." Morgan went on to explain the concept of reincarnation, which originated with the Hindu religion. It taught that all life forms are souls at various stages of development, and when they die they will be born in another life form, depending upon how they had lived in their previous life. This meant that people could conceivably die and return to the life cycle as an animal. I reasoned that my deceased grandma might come back as a cow and end up on my table! Once I thought that through, I decided meat eating wasn't for me.

The day I told Mom that I wanted to be a vegetarian, she panicked. "You will lose all your *energy*!" she cried, "You won't get enough protein!" But it was hopeless. Mom knew that once I had set my mind on something, it was useless to try to dissuade me. "Don't worry, Mom. I'll be just fine." I said. Then I went on to live on a diet so unbalanced it should have killed me.

Not knowing a thing about how to cook vegetarian food didn't help. I ate iceberg lettuce salads with Thousand Island dressing every night for dinner, and the remainder of the time subsisted on little more than sugar. Because of my job at Jorgenson's candy store, I had free access to the bins of chocolates, jelly beans, hard candy and gumdrops. I should have died of sugar overdose or become a blimp, but I remained thin and healthy. Such is youth.

It was discovered that I had a curvature of the spine, and the osteopath told me to get a book on Yoga and do the exercises to strengthen my back. At first I was repelled by the idea, but eventually I got the book and read it from cover to cover. From that point forward, I read any and everything I could get my hands on that had to do with Hinduism or meditation. A woman who taught Yoga came as a special guest to my social studies class. I ended up studying with her and went on to become a Yoga instructor while I was still in my teens. Vegetarianism and other alternate life styles were not as fashionable as they are today, and so I began to be known as "that girl who is into weird stuff" around the school. Some were intrigued, some were intimidated, and my mom's born-again Christian friend, Mrs. Starr, was beside herself.

"You're into *what*? Jennifer, don't you know that all those religions are from the *devil*?" she scolded. We sat at a table at the country club both of our families belonged to, she in her tennis skirt after a game with the ladies and me in a bathing suit after augmenting my tan.

"Don't worry about it, Mrs. Starr. It's really helping me!" I chirped.

"*Helping* you!" this lady had an edge to her voice sharp enough to cut through the sandwich she was eating. "What do you do when you . . . meditate?" That word didn't come out of her mouth easily.

"I envision a golden light going through my body, and just relax and try to empty my mind of clutter," I said.

"And what is this *golden light*?" she crooned, narrowing her eyes into slits.

"It's . . . God, I guess," I shrugged.

"Well, at the church I go to, they teach us how all that stuff is from the devil. I think you should really just take the religion your parents raised you with to be safe," she intoned.

My heart closed like a clam to her prying advice. Thinking back,

I realize that she would have had more effect if she had listened more than talked. I had been disillusioned—and rightly so—by Christianity, but no one had ever asked me why. Then here this lady was trying to tell me that breathing deeply and seeing golden light was evil. I was searching outside of Christianity because the church had failed me, and I wouldn't listen to Christians unless they were honest about their failures.

❦ ❦ ❦ ❦

I shopped for answers like most girls my age shopped for clothes. My search into religions and philosophies continued with increasing intensity. One pseudo-New Age organization I stumbled upon, called "Arica Institute," put on a weekend seminar. Arica was founded by Oscar Ichazo, a student of Zen, Sufism, Yoga, Buddhism, Confucianism, I Ching and Jewish Mysticism. Ichazo had his first training in 1971 in Arica, Chili, and from there the organization flourished around the world.

Their weekend training promised enlightenment and spiritual freedom. I believed that God, whoever He or She was, would lead through the opportunities of life, and the opportunity to attend this event presented itself through a friend named Amy. Amy was a girl far more sophisticated than her sixteen years, and seemed to be as earnest as I was to discover what was missing in life. At the Arica training, Amy and I had a weekend I will never forget.

We were the youngest of the all-women group. About a dozen of us gathered in a large, bare room for "psychocalistentics" which were exercises that purported to use physical movement to free a person from "fixations," such as overeating and anger. The sessions were rigorous beyond what I expected, and the instructors were cold and unfriendly. There was an almost glazed look in their eyes that was presumably supposed to indicate inner peace and detachment.

The exhausting day was followed by a second day even more difficult, and the finale of the weekend was an exercise where one person stared into the opposite eye of the other until a certain feeling of oneness with that person was felt. I ended up being paired with a lesbian woman who felt deeply connected with me after that. I have to admit that it made me nervous.

Returning home after the Arica weekend, I was a changed person. I had felt to the core the essence of existential philosophy, which basically said, "There is no personal God, no reason for living, just a cold infinity beyond your insignificant life." Once a TV-aholic, I began to abstain from all TV except a show on public television by a Zen Buddhist named Alan Watts. He combined Zen and the existential philosophy of a contemporary French philosopher named Jean-Paul Sartre. The goal of both of these schools was to lead an austere, passive existence, but one that was emphatically atheist. I had always believed that there was a God, and this new idea produced a certain depression that my mother noticed. Good old mom came into the TV room one day where I had just watched Alan Watts. I had turned the TV off and was sitting in silence, drinking oriental tea, staring into space and trying to "just be."

"Jennifer!" she screeched. "What are you doing? You are acting so strange lately! What has gotten into you?" I couldn't understand why she didn't see the spiritual progress I was making.

"Oh, Mom, I'm fine!" I retorted, "What's wrong with just sitting here? Would you be happier if I was watching 'Leave It to Beaver?' " But mom had an intuitive reason to be concerned for me in my existential phase. Depression that results from an incorrect belief system can be lethal. I went on to ultimately find the true happiness that comes from Jesus Christ, but I can't say the same for Amy, who committed suicide only a short time later.

❦ ❦ ❦ ❦

My search into eastern religions became more bizarre with every venture. Someone told me of an ashram in the city where there were Sikhs (pronounced "Zeeks"), a certain type of Hindu that practiced a severe discipline called Kundalini Yoga. A group of about twenty or so Sikhs lived in an otherwise typical neighborhood, wearing their turbans and white robes everywhere they went from the post office and the grocery store. Once a week they would open up the house for guests and conduct an hour-long exercise and meditation session that rivaled Olympic training.

When a friend and I attended once, we were led to do two hundred deep-knee bends in rapid succession without stopping. After that we were to hold perfectly still with our eyes closed and follow the guru (leader) as he guided us in a meditation. I peeked at him as we sat there, and thought, "He is really kind of diabolical!" His piercing blue eyes rolled back into his cloth-wrapped head as he talked about karma and enlightenment. Every once in a while during exercises his voice would dip into a low shout and he would bark, "Just DO IT!!" after which everyone would push harder on their tired bodies. He seemed to have total control over the people who lived there, giving orders in the matter-of-fact way of a military general. They had some kind of moral code for the ashram, but it was one that accommodated his polygamy. Even I thought it was a weird place.

❦❦❦❦

The basic goal of all of these religions and practices was summed up in the word "enlightenment." This was allegedly a state of surrender in which the person became one with the cosmic essence some called "God." Once that blissful oneness was achieved, the desires of the body would no longer clamor for satisfaction—that's what they said, anyway. And it sounded just like what I needed. My addictive personality was always seeking escape through some temporary anesthesia; alcohol, food, tobacco, parties, friends or drugs. These were the all-too open doors that beckoned me like desert mirages. I longed to be a whole person, free of the chains that had already tethered my young heart, but nothing seemed to work.

Driven to extremes, I would party into the wee hours of Saturday night, then wake up Sunday morning to watch the sunrise over Lake Michigan while I did deep breathing to get the tar from Camel Straights out of my lungs. One night I was at a Frank Zappa concert and a few nights later I was at choir practice with my mom. I refused to eat meat, but I was willing to take street drugs. God was a question mark, and life was a pointless paradox.

In my experimentation with New Age disciplines, I was willing to endure great privations, yet I had no true self-control. This is the twisted thing about legalism. The greater the effort to save yourself, the more self-focused you become. The more self-focused you become, the further you are from salvation. The cycle of self whirls around and around until you are dizzy with exasperation. I am sure that God felt my dizziness along with me.

There was a time in His ministry when Jesus looked out upon a crowd of world-weary people just like me and said,

> "Come to Me, all who are weary and heavy-laden, and I will give you rest. Take My yoke upon you, and learn from Me, for I am gentle and humble in heart; and YOU SHALL FIND REST FOR YOUR SOULS. For My yoke is easy, and My load is light" (Matthew 11:28-30, NAS).

I was weary and heavy-laden with my strenuous disciplines and exercises. The ages hold stories of millions like me, from Hindu devotees to Catholic monks, who tried to be saved the hard way and failed. Pride keeps so many from accepting the way that Jesus said was "easy." I am sure Jesus saw me toiling away and wished I would come to Him and find rest . . . but He knew I wasn't quite ready.

❦❦❦❦

There's a stark, rocky ledge in the den of decay
Where the wolves yell and yammer and clamor for prey
And the wandering lambs quiver helplessly there
Thinking they're out of the kind Shepherd's care
There's a sound in the bush and a form that appears
With eyes that are never quite empty of tears
And a voice that rings caring and love in the ears
Caring and love in the ears
And the Shepherd heads home as the wind blows colder
And I am the lamb on His shoulder
I am the lamb on His shoulder

There's a wound in the heart of the infinite sky
That never quite heals as time scratches by
And it weeps 'oer the likes of you and of me
And the salt in the sore is our apathy
There's a wizened old Sage and He's pointing the way
And He aches when so much as a thought goes astray
And searches for wanderers day after day
Searching for day after day
And the Shepherd heads home as the wind blows colder
And I am the lamb on His shoulder
I am the lamb on His shoulder

From the song "The Lamb on His Shoulder" on the CD *Banish the Myth*. Copyright 1995, Jennifer Jill Schwirzer.

❦❦❦❦

CHAPTER 5

Spiritual Alternatives

In a beautiful house in Bayside, Wisconsin, a dark-haired woman walked into the master bedroom. Her husband lay on the king-sized bed in his cotton pajamas, reading a newspaper. The woman sighed, trying to get the man's attention, but the man didn't seem to notice. The woman sighed again, louder this time, almost in a whine, but with the same results. Finally she said out loud, "Did you hear the latest?"

"What latest?" the man didn't take his eyes off the paper.

"Jennifer wants to go to some obscure little college in Michigan for the summer," the woman said.

"Oh?" The man was asking for more information in his own way.

"And she wants to go with that mime she met at Theater X," the woman moaned.

Now the man's interest was thoroughly aroused. Laying aside the paper, he squinted up at the woman and puzzled, "What, pray tell, is a mime? And what in the world is Theater X?"

❦❦❦❦

The political upheaval of the sixties gave way to a quieter decade during which the Vietnam War ended, and the attention of many was turned inward. Self-development was the main entree, social activism more of a side dish.

But there was still general malice on the part of the young people toward the established older generation. The questioning of social mores that began in the sixties was still playing itself out into the seventies. Judeo-Christian beliefs were being set aside for the more exotic eastern religions. Alternative schools and lifestyles were a fascination. And I was right in step. Nonconformity became a way of life for me. I was willing to try anything that presented itself, as long as it promised to be a better option than the norm.

One of the "alternative" forms of education that came along was something called "the house." It was my high school's desperate attempt to interest students in social studies at a time when they were flunking history by the droves. Probably the disillusionment that Vietnam and Watergate had injected into the youth was to blame for their apathy. "Why study a government that has botched everything so completely?" we asked. "Why study the history of a nation that sends its young men off to a pointless jungle war?"

"The house" was just that—a house slightly off campus that lent itself to a more informal, relaxed style of learning. The students were allowed to design their own course of study, and encouraged to facilitate discussion, or "rap" groups with other students on issues that they thought relevant. The concept was revolutionary, but the application of it was a joke. For most students, "the house" was an easy way to avoid Mr. Beaterman's *boooorring* American history lectures and the pressure of tests and term papers.

This was a school filled with spoiled upper-middle-class brats who thought they ruled, and they often did. This was a school where a drug-soaked, longhaired student council actually got the board to approve of a student smoking lounge! They were not about to study when they didn't have to, and so "the house" became an excellent place to recover from yesterday's LSD trip. It was a bonafide crash pad for scholastic defectors, and everyone went there to vegetate.

Everyone but me.

I saw the house as an opportunity to pursue my search for truth. Among other studies, I researched life after death. The spirit of God was surging into my mind and bringing forth a groundswell of questions on the essential issues of life. I wasn't content to live unaware of what would become of me, or anyone, after death, and so I hunted for a clear, believable answer.

I read Elizabeth Kuubler-Ross and interviewed everyone from my father, an agnostic, to my Christian Scientist grandmother. Sadly, though I heard and read many interesting theories, I was not shown the simple biblical truth that death was a sleep from which we would wake at the coming of Jesus (1 Thessalonians 4:16,17). No one told me that eternal life depended upon our union with Jesus Christ, who alone had immortality (1 Timothy 6:16). Still, God used this time of searching to prepare me to appreciate those truths once I did find them. In fact, once I discovered the biblical truth years later, I went back to share it with Mr. Arnott, my teacher.

"Well, how has life been since you graduated?" he asked, surprised to see me.

"Great, Mr. Arnott! I have become a born-again Christian." I announced.

"Oh . . ." his eyes shadowed over.

"Do you remember that unit I did on life after death?" I asked.

"Sure," he answered with a sheepish look.

"Well, I have discovered the truth! We don't live immediately after death, we go to sleep until Jesus comes, at which point He will call us from the grave and we will go on to live forever with Him!" I explained jubilantly (2 Thessalonians 4:15-18).

Poor Mr. Arnott was not prepared for my impromptu sermon. No doubt he thought that my nights of drug experimentation had finally taken their toll.

During another period at the house, I studied the Catholic activist Mike Culligan. He and a group of protesters had broken into the federal building in downtown Milwaukee during the Vietnam War and burned thousands of draft cards. In researching his life and work, I was brought in contact with a man named Ken Feit (pronounced like "fight") who had known Culligan. Feit was an ex-Jesuit priest who had joined an underground theater in the city where I saw him perform as a mime. My boyfriend and I went to his home for the Culligan interview. After getting the information I needed about Culligan, he told me about an "alternative" college he taught at in Michigan, which snagged my interest because senior year was rolling around, and I had no idea what I was going to do.

And that was a very serious problem. My parents had raised us to be goal-oriented and ambitious. In their younger years, they had struggled against depression-era odds and squeezed out a college education for themselves. Dad spent his last $300 on Mom's wedding ring and their first apartment was down the hall from a shared bathroom. From there Dad climbed the corporate ladder, working twelve hour days and spending one week in three out of town on business. No child of theirs was going to endure the humiliation they had known, they vowed. No need for it! Their daughter was going to a nice, reputable college!

Ha.

Little did they conceive of the malcontent that was brewing in their seventeen-year-old's world. I didn't know what I wanted, but I knew what I didn't want, and I *didn't* want the norm. I was repulsed by status quo, allergic to tradition. I believed somewhere beneath the part of me that could speak, that there was something out there that would satisfy all my hungers. And I knew that this something was off, *way* off the beaten path. Mom packed me up into her station wagon and we cruised around the Midwest looking at all the best schools. I could pick where I wanted to go, she said, nothing was out of the question. But my heart sunk a league deeper with each campus tour as I realized that the pull away from protocol was drawing me beyond what my parents could understand.

At this time, my conception of God—though it existed—was as unclear as a road sign in the fog. I didn't know if God was a He or a She, a friend or a force field. But I did have one thing straight. I believed God had a place for me, a place where I would be set like a jewel in a crown. And I had not found that place yet.

As graduation loomed, my mom and dad's worry for me tightened into a knot. I wasn't any more reassured than they were. It was a tough time for me, having to decide if I would pursue my search for truth or fall into step with the herd and be safe. I was shocked as one by one my friends with whom I had fantasized about going "back to the land" decided they would go to college instead. I was forced to stand totally alone. Even my relationship with Rick faded into gray as we came to the fork in the road. He took the well-traveled-route of convention and I . . .well, I took the road less traveled by.

When the "where are you going after graduation?" question got unbearably hard to answer, I remembered the "progressive" school Ken Feit told me about. There was the perfect answer to my dilemma. My parents could have the comfort of knowing I was in college, but I would have the freedom to study what I wanted to study. This school, called Thomas Jefferson College, offered the same self-designed curriculum option that "the house" had offered. This would be my chance to search for the truth and get credit for it, pleasing my parents and me at the same time.

❦ ❦ ❦ ❦

Mom had given up on my being normal by now, and she kind of nodded numbly as I explained, "I want to go to a summer course called 'Spiritual Alternatives.' It's in Michigan. I'll probably end up staying there for freshman year. It's a progressive program, Mom, just the kind I thrive in."

"How did you hear about this school?" Mom sighed.

"I met this guy named Ken Feit who performs for Theater X." I knew that would score some points with Mom because she had once been an actress and loved the theater.

"So you would go with him to Michigan?" she asked.

"Yeah, on the bus. It's a two-day ride. We'd stay at his friend's house in Chicago." I tried to sound cheerful.

"Do you know anything about this man?" she puzzled.

"Yeah, sure. He used to be a Jesuit priest, and now he does theater full time. He performs at 'Theater X,' as a mime among other things. He's really an interesting person." I said.

"I'll bet," she said, no doubt remembering all my other "interesting" friends.

By the end of our conversation, Mom knew that I planned to take a bus with a man more than twice my age who had been a Jesuit but was now a mime to a school that had no grades where he would be teaching a summer class about spiritual alternatives.

Mom said, "OK."

I was shocked that she didn't object to my boarding a bus with a man I hardly knew and she *didn't* know. But now I realize Mom was exhausted from raising me for almost eighteen years.

❦❦❦❦

You live in wealth of many kinds
You know the thinking of the finest minds
You've read the books, you know the words
You've talked to those who've heard the things you have heard
But what about the people of Ninevah?

You're life is tidy as a pin
You have so many things to put on your skin
You love to sell, you love to buy
You love to laugh, you don't want to cry
But what about the people of Ninevah?

You go to church dressed like a star
All of the pretty people know who you are
You say a prayer, you sing a song
You hope the preacher won't talk too long
But what about the people of Ninevah?

Are things as perfect as they seem?
You worked so hard to get your picture perfect dream
Your house on sand will never last
Your microcosm is fading fast
For what about the people of Ninevah?

❦❦❦❦

CHAPTER 6

The Dancer

Fall, 1975.

Grand Valley State College in Allendale, Michigan was silent and dark for the most part except for one building, which was filled with partying women. What started out as a feminist rally had turned into a rowdy dance. Oldies' music pulsated until the walls shook while women stomped and spun around with one another, laughing and teaching each other steps. Dark angles with twisted bodies danced alongside of them, even as a company of pure, holy angels stood outside, looking with solicitude into the windows.

A sweaty girl with long wavy hair burst out of the front door and onto the steps, sighing with relief as the cold night air hit her lungs. A group of women and girls clustered around the steps, some clasping hands and holding one another affectionately. The girl tenuously sat near them, laying her head back on the railing and gazing up at the stars. She felt drawn and repulsed by these women at the same time. She wanted to belong, but she wasn't a lesbian, and wasn't planning on becoming one. As she stared imperviously at the sky, one of the older women reached over and began stroking her brow.

❦❦❦❦

The summer course was a strange adventure for all of us. I don't remember "learning" much, but I met hoards of people who were involved in the eastern religions, the occult, or some other alternative lifestyle. It was a fascinating world I had entered, full of people who were just as offbeat as I was.

I settled into a house full of students and promptly fell in love with a boy named Steve. Blessed with a very brilliant mind, he was easy to be enamored with. Add to that the fact that he was a dead-ringer for the western version of Jesus, with long sandy brown hair and gray eyes. I would sit for hours and listen to his friends and him howl Bob Dylan tunes. None of them could really sing, but they thundered away on their guitars as if they were performing at Woodstock. I was too scared to sing in front of them, but I would think, "What's so great about Bob Dylan?" and I would go write my own little confused songs in the privacy of my room.

The summer passed quickly for me, and I decided to stay at the school for the following year. Unfortunately, my parents insisted that I live in student housing. I begged them to let me live off campus in one of the farmhouses that groups of students rented, but they said no, and they were paying the bills at that point.

Oh, but I hated student housing. I lived with three other young women in an apartment with two bedrooms, a bath and a kitchen. I was the only vegetarian, so there was little sharing of food. But worse than that, the other girls were terrible slobs. Stacks of grease-caked dishes stood in the sink for days at a time. I would beg, plead, bargain, but to no avail.

That was one of the unpleasant things I had to face about going to Thomas Jefferson College for the year, but otherwise I felt quite at home. This school was an experimental branch of a state college, drawing other searching people like me, so I fit in well with what was sometimes quite a freak show.

All of the female teachers at the school were militant lesbian feminists. I had a growing interest in feminism, but I wasn't ready to change my "orientation." Still, I was drawn to their meetings because I felt accepted there. I sensed that some of the teachers wanted to "convert" me to their lifestyle and I have to admit that in some ways it was an appealing offer. For once in my life I didn't have to be pretty, popular, or otherwise exceptional in order to be accepted. I just had to be female, and that I was.

I believe that many of the groups that people join operate on the same dynamic. Under the guise of a worthy cause, people collect into groups, not really because of their passion for the cause but because they want to be part of something bigger than themselves. We all naturally yearn to be part of a power structure. When we can't find that acceptance in the community, the family, the church, we try to find it in divergent groups. Even today I don't share the repulsion toward gay people that some Christians seem to have. Divergent sexual practices are just an outward manifestation of inward emptiness. I know that many of the lesbian women on my college campus were just seeking for love and thinking they had found it.

❦ ❦ ❦ ❦

My next discovery was dance. I had always loved the art of movement. Often at parties, I would break into dance while peers stared self-consciously on. Now I had the opportunity of turning my natural gift into a profession. Many of the young people who trained at this school went on to join modern dance troops in New York. The idea of doing something creative, communicative and musical was right up my alley.

Soon I was running around with a group of dancers. Every event was an opportunity to dance, from a walk in the park when we danced to the sound of the crickets, to the nights when we congregated in someone's living room and danced as a group in one huge human clump. Hours were spent isolating muscles and finding new ways to move. The professional teachers that came in had musculature on their bodies that prize athletes would only dream of. Much of the choreography was beautiful and graceful, and oh, I wanted to learn. "I have finally found it," I wrote to my mom. "This is what I have been looking for all my life."

But in spite of the fulfillment I felt in the dancing arena, I was lonely as ever. I felt trapped in the small apartment, so I determined to answer an ad to sublet a farmhouse about a mile down the road. I needed a place to be alone and think over my direction in life, and this sounded perfect. Believing that God, whoever She was (I was leaning toward a matriarchal God-concept at this point—probably because of all those feminists!), would lead me to where I needed to be in order to facilitate my spiritual journey. I jumped on my ten-speed bike and sped down the road.

It was a mild winter day, and a light snow had just fallen. Normally the country roads in Allendale were pocketed with ridges that would slow any biker to a crawl, but the snow had filled all those ridges in, and I sailed as if on glass to the address on my card. I perceived this as God telling me that I was being guided to the place I was meant to be. I jumped off my bike in a breathless wonder at the quiet old house and the huge barn that seemed to stare back at me in a benign welcome.

I then did what any self-respecting Zen Buddhist (that's as close as I can get to describing what I was at that point) would do when confronted with a divine providence—I bowed. I bowed to the house; I bowed to the barn. I bowed out of reverence for discovering what I knew was in "the plan" for me, and I bowed out of sheer joy that I would have a room of my own and an escape from piles of pot roast-coated dishes. Boy, was I happy!

The people in the house were smiling, too—in hysterical laughter at the fruitcake outside who was bowing to inanimate buildings! But they were not strangers to my way of thinking. One of them, named Butch, moved out of the room that I moved into and left the book *Autobiography of a Yogi* which I quickly read in a few sittings. Another fellow named Brian was a thin, sensitive young man with a bush of brown hair and kind eyes who considered himself a spiritual seeker as well. I signed all the necessary papers to sublet the house with three other young women, and said goodbye to Brian and Butch, not realizing that I would see them again.

Oh, how I loved my country farmhouse and my quiet, austere little room. Every day I would jump out of bed and plop down cross-legged next to my terrarium on the floor. Closing my eyes, I would breathe steady and deep as I counted on amethyst beads my grandmother had given me. I felt I could not start my day without seeking God. I had devised my own meditation, feeling it was as good as any. Many young people learned their meditation techniques from a guru, some even buying a mantra* from Guru Maharaji's organization. They were told that this would enhance their chances of finding enlight-

---

* A mantra is a word used in meditation, repeated over and over, often producing a hypnotic effect.

enment. But I believed that if there was a God, and it really *was* possible to reach enlightenment, it would be free of charge. So once more the original self-starter did things her own way.

I was more faithful to my discipline of meditation than many Christians are to prayer. I was willing to subject myself to hardship and deprivation in order to pursue spiritual freedom. Devotees in Zen monasteries live on rice gruel and salty broth, meditating day and night, sleeping on straw mats. Disciples of Hinduism fast to the point of starvation, living as hermits in caves. Such rigorous effort we humans are capable of, and all so that we can take some credit for "making it" on our own. I sought God, and I did not find Him because pride blinded me to the fact that He was seeking me.

There is no account in the Bible of a lost sheep seeking the shepherd—it's the other way around, and for a reason. God is seeking us, each one of us, but our natural impulse is to avoid Him. "The sinner . . . may refuse to be drawn to Christ; but if he does not resist he will be drawn to Jesus" (*Steps to Christ*, p. 27). Really, "finding God" is a matter of ceasing to run from Him. At this point in my blind groping, I was still not ready to receive the Lord.

But I was getting there.

❦ ❦ ❦ ❦

Ken Feit reappeared on the scene, running a weekend course for a group of students on his favorite subject—spiritual alternatives—this time with an emphasis on world religions. Ken announced to us that we would be spending the weekend locked in a classroom building. We would be researching further into spiritual paths, learning from books, from our own meditations and from one another, but we were not permitted to talk or eat.

I had fasted before. A high school social studies teacher showed us live footage of the holocaust once, then recommended that we observe a day of fasting and mourning. I don't think anyone refused. Then there were "world food days" when my boyfriend and I decided to fast in order to empathize with the starving millions. He wimped out by the end of the day, but I had no problem. I had fasted often as part of my yoga routine.

The refraining from talking was a bit more out of the ordinary for me. I have to admit it was a strange experience to be with a bunch of people and not talk. Sign language, writing, and eye contact would have to be enough.

I went into the weekend with the determination to find the truth I had been looking for. Sitting in a group of tomb-silent people with spirits as scrambled as mine, I felt my desperate condition. Tears streamed down my face as I hoped that I would find "it" this weekend. "It" had eluded me thus far, in spite of my increasingly strenuous pursuit, but I felt now I was closing in on the prize. Would it turn out to be Zen Buddhism? Taoism? Hinduism? Gestalt therapy? I had no clue, I just knew there was something out there that I would find someday.

I don't remember much about the three-day vigil except the finale. Ken directed us to smear on "white face," which was clown makeup, and once we were coated, we danced around the building, performing mime stunts and generally acting out our confusion. After that we ate and talked, thinking we had experienced some kind of spiritual renewal, but in fact we came out of the weekend more lost than we had gone in.

❦❦❦❦

Psychology was my next obsession. This branch of medicine, previously thought to be for the mentally ill only, began mainstreaming in the seventies. "Normal" people were incorporating group and individual therapy into their lives. I attended every class and read every book I could find in hopes of finding a balm to assuage my loneliness. Dream therapy told me to write down my dreams, which were interesting but non-revelatory. Group therapy advocated sitting in groups where individuals confronted one another, often grinding each other down with criticism. This hardly seemed beneficial. "Rolfing" was a type of painful, deep massage that purported to dig into a person's emotional disorders while causing excruciating physical pain. There was even something called "scream therapy". A friend of mine named Billy had done it. He seemed as messed up as anyone I knew, but when

I met Kris, a man who had also undergone a session, I decided to let him tell me about it.

"It's really intense," Kris said, drawing on a Camel cigarette through a clenched jaw. "But I know it's the way to freedom."

"What was it like?" I asked.

"You spend several hours with the therapist," he said, "and they guide you through a series of screams. You are screaming out all the pain of your life, starting with the most recent and going back, back, back to your childhood. Finally you get back to the first traumatic moment you had as a baby, and you scream the primal scream. Boy, it's really quite an experience. I have never screamed so loud and so long in my . . ."

"So what good does it do you?" I butted in.

"Well . . ." he stammered, blowing out Camel smoke, "It's hard to tell. I just know that they said that once all the pain was released, all my emotional damage would be healed, and I would be a whole person."

I looked at Kris. Probably about twenty-five, he looked twice his age. His skin was deeply lined, his eyes shadowed. Chain-smoking and unable to smile or laugh, I knew that primal scream therapy had not done him much good.

❦❦❦❦

Cries from the valley
God answers many such prayers
"I will be with you," He says
"All through your worst nightmares."
But there was one prayer
Cried by the Son He held dear
God was strangely silent then
It was as if He did not hear

Anathema! It was midnight as the sun refused to shine
Anathema! And Justice gave a nod
Anathema! When you think of all the things you've left behind
Will you remember the God-forsaken God?

From the song "Anathema; the God-Forsaken God" on the CD *Chance of Rain.*

❦❦❦❦

CHAPTER 7

Loneliness Catches Up

W*inter, 1975.*

At the door of a ramshackle farmhouse in Allendale, Michigan stood a tall young man with a mop of black hair. Glancing over his shoulder, he knocked nervously until a young woman's form filled the door. Light splashed out into the yard as the door flew open, the two embraced briefly, and the man entered.

Behind an unseen veil, bright angels created a wall of defense against the dark angels that had sought to prevent the man from entering. A cloud of cursing rose from their fiendish mouths as the two battalions wrestled mightily. Finally the dark angels weakened, and one by one they turned away from the holy angels, who stood like white-clad soldiers around the door. The last angel to give up the fight was a wretched creature with a twisted face. Walking into the night, he turned to his heavenly opponents with one last dig:

"She'll never listen to him. She hates Jesus, and she always will."

❦❦❦❦

Norman was a whimsical fellow in one of my dance classes. He was as clumsy as an ox, but he had a certain childlike charm that I liked. We began spending time together. The only thing that seemed to stand in the way of a solid relationship between us was his girlfriend, Christine, who was away in New York City for several weeks studying dance. Christine must have been a special person, I thought, but what will she think of me?

Soon enough I found out. In the shower one day after dance class, I noticed a girl I had never seen before. She was enjoying the echo created by the large multi-nozzeled stall by singing away like a choirboy, and I joined her, adding to the symphony. Soon we were laughing together, perfect strangers, enjoying the serendipity of the moment. With a smile she turned to me.

"Jennifer?"

"Christine?" I asked, knowing what the answer would be. From that moment forward we were friends, no twinge of jealousy ever showing itself. I decided that since she was such a nice girl, she could have Norman. (Not that I had a choice!)

The two of them lived in another farmhouse in a nearby town with several other students. Eventually I lost contact with Norman until one night some months later when he showed up at my door, his face white as chalk and fear clawing in his voice.

"I have to talk to you," he whispered, the usual sunlight gone from his face. He followed me to the stairs that led to my room and we sat while he talked between ragged breaths.

"A man named Karl is living at our farm house. No one really knows him that well, but somehow he got permission to stay with us for a while. He is just sort of hanging around now, really causing problems. He seems to be demon possessed, you know, saying weird things and burning himself with fire and . . ." he gulped, "threatening people. It gets worse and worse until we say the name of 'Jesus,' and then he stops and the evil spirit leaves."

Conviction tapped on my shoulder, but instead of whirling around to face it, I fought. *No, no, not Jesus, not Christianity,* I thought. I had already tried it and found it to be a dead end. Nothing more than a bunch of moralistic people trying to impose unnatural constraints upon the culture. I had moved on from the stodgy traditions of the western world to the exotic religions of the east . . .

"Oh, come on!" I spoke up, "Believe in God, but *Jesus*? I don't think we have to resort to that!"

"I didn't either, but we were scared enough to try anything. Christine remembered reading in the Bible how Jesus used to cast out demons, and so we gave it a try, and it worked! Maybe Jesus *is* the answer after all. Maybe He *is* God, and all this other stuff we have been doing . . ."

"No, no, it can't be." I shook my head in refusal. In spite of the plain evidence Norman was giving that Jesus was the source of power over evil, my heart was a stone in my chest. The idea of Christianity repulsed me, with all it's pretension and hypocrisy. I had grown up in a church-going family, in a Christian culture, and I had left it all to find "the truth." Now I was being told that the power was in Jesus Christ.

Where was this powerful Jesus, I wondered, when the children in Bangladesh starved while the "Christians" in America wallowed in excess? Where was this powerful Jesus when the church spent more money on a new organ than they spent on charity? Why couldn't this powerful Jesus make "real" people out of the plastic professed Christians I had met? Cynicism blinded my eyes to the truth. No way would I regress back to Christianity, I thought. I was on a spiritual path that would someday lead to enlightenment if I tried hard enough. I wasn't giving up now—for Jesus, for anyone!

❦ ❦ ❦ ❦

Then there was Al. He must have weighed about ninety pounds, but otherwise I remember him looking almost exactly like Jerry Seinfeld, complete with the nasal New York accent. Having rejected his native Judaism like I had rejected Christianity, we were in about the same place, which was basically everywhere and nowhere at the same time. "Let's try this!" We would say, and paint our faces like clowns, traipsing around the campus and performing mime stunts. "Now let's try this," we'd decide, and whirl like the Muslim whirling dervishes staring at the horizon.

It was Al who first introduced me to the occult, offering to read my tarot cards.* I agreed, willing to try everything, but reluctant to involve

---

* Tarot cards are a set of picture cards from which evolved our common playing cards. These are spread by a "reader" before a person seeking special knowledge about themselves. The reader then interprets the cards for the inquirer, in much the same way a palm reader reads into an inquirer's life.

myself in the black arts because of the negativity associated with them. I don't recall much about the tarot card reading he did except that when it was over, I walked out to the hall and collapsed to the floor, closing my eyes. It seemed at that moment that my whole life flashed before me in a few seconds, rushing by like a locomotive in blazing color and sound. I was left totally drained of energy and emotion, feeling almost overwhelming insignificance. It was one more remarkable experience, but still no answer. My life was a whirl of activity and exoticism. In my mind I was making progress toward my goal, but really I was a lost lamb.

❦ ❦ ❦ ❦

One weekend after Norman's visit I went to a women's retreat at a private residence. It was to be a meeting of all the feminist minds on the campus—teachers and students included. Entering the house, I felt an exhilarating energy. The music of Joni Mitchell blared as various people sang along with her:

Don't interrupt the sorrow/Darn right/In flames our prophet witches/Be polite/Anima rising/Queen of Queens/Wash my guilt of Eden/Wash and balance me/Truth goes up in vapors/The steeples lean/Winds of change patriarchs/Snug in your bible belt dreams/God goes up the chimney/Like childhood Santa Claus/The good slaves love the good book/A rebel loves a cause.

The song was a feminist anthem full of imagery that villainized Christianity and glorified mythology and the occult. Step by step, I had been led to a frame of mind where these things were right and true. I had never read the Bible for myself, but I believed the lie that it was actually to blame for the oppression of women.

Little did I know that Jesus Christ did more to restore women's rights than any other figure in human history. He was not primarily a social reformer, yet His life and death would do more than any revolution could toward the restoration of all human rights because He paid an infinite price for each soul. In Jesus, and because of Him, each person has value beyond estimation. He lived in accordance with this fact, treating outcasts, which women were in biblical times, with respect and love. He traveled with women (Luke 8:1-3), had friendships with women (Luke

10:38,39), and even allowed Mary to anoint Him, head to foot, recommending that her act be reported right along with His gospel (Luke 7:37-39, John 11:2, Matthew 26:13). Most significantly, He exposed the crime of sexual abuse of women (Luke 7:40-47).

But for that weekend my mind was enveloped in darkness with a fortress full of soldiers who had a cause to love and an enemy to hate.

❦❦❦❦

Enlightenment, or Nirvana, or God, or whatever I was looking for was soon to be found, I vowed, summoning up my will. I resolved to do whatever it took to get there. Enough of trying to be a student in a school and pursue my spiritual aim at the same time. It was time, I felt, to make a clean break and go live somewhere with a group of people who were as serious about spiritual things as I was, devoting one hundred percent of the time to meditation.

Someone gave me a catalogue of such communities all over the United States. These were often called "ashrams" or "monasteries" and were basically collections of people that had placed themselves under the tutelage of a "guru" or "master," someone who had pursued the discipline for many years. Each entry in the catalogue had a description of the place and a picture of the leader on the opposite page.

As I leafed through the book, I got a glimpse of the kind of men I would be learning from if I made the choice to go. What a remarkable array of oddballs they were! One was pencil-thin, dressed only in a loincloth. The next had a white beard down to his knees. One looked almost normal, except that his eyes were rolled back into his head as if he was having convulsions. The next one was corpulent and wore a huge white turban. The next one was twisted into a knot like a contortionist in a circus sideshow. I couldn't take it. I slammed the book shut, and spoke out loud.

"I'm weird, but not this weird!"

❦❦❦❦

I knew a young student who was a disciple of a certain Indian Guru in the area. One day this young woman, named Kiree, put on a concert of Indian chant music that she had learned from this man. As her bony arms struck her autoharp, her nasal voice sang words no one understood. She was supposedly happy and spiritually fulfilled, but as I watched her I felt pity. Talking to her later confirmed my fears that her life with her teacher was not even normal, much less happy. He had a strange dictatorial control over her, as if she had no will of her own—and yet she accepted this as part of her "path." I could not imagine putting myself in a similar situation. I was going to have to find God myself!

At this point my belief in reincarnation was almost unshakable. I remember distinctly meeting people whom I felt I had some mystical connection with. Even total strangers I would sometimes approach with, "I . . . I think I knew you in a past life!"

And they would agree!

But as confident as I was with all my beliefs, as disciplined as I was with my regimen, as earnest as I was in my journey, all it took was a moment of truth to tell me I had nothing. Usually that moment came on a Friday night when I had nowhere in particular to go. No party to attend, no classes to run to, I would sit in my quiet little farmhouse and feel the loneliness come crashing in.

This was not just a generic, bored, longing-for-company type of loneliness, it was a loneliness that bore down like an avalanche, covering me without mercy in a blanket so dark I felt I would smother. It was a loneliness I had fled for years, running every time it came close to me—to another book, another event, another relationship. I pictured it as an old man who spoke softly through his beard, patronizing me with the knowledge of my doom. It was this overwhelming loneliness that kept me pushing forward in my search for truth.

I did not realize that what I felt was part of my human condition. The Bible tells us that we are all separated from God, "alienated and hostile in mind, engaged in evil deeds" (Colossians 1:21, NAS). I thought this revelation of my solitude was something particular to me, and as I observed my comrades in their folly and laughter I would wonder how they could be so happy. Actually, the same alienation was buried inside of them. God in His wisdom knew that I was ready to begin opening my eyes to my true condition. Soon He would show me more of my dark, isolated self, and He would show me Jesus, who had "made peace through the blood of His cross" (v. 20).

❦❦❦❦

Here is the face
Here is the grin
Peel back the laughter
Look deep within
Long I have known the life that you lead
You try to hide it, but you don't succeed

Look at me now, tell what you see
I was as broken as one could be
Not any more, the good news is true
The only thing is, I want the same for you

I can see it in your eyes, you've lost your way
Like a child without a mother, like a ship without a bay
Like a soldier with no country, like a lamb without a fold
You wander in your heartbreak with loneliness untold
I can see it in your past, the things they did
That said you were a loser ever since you were a kid
And if memories could listen, I'd tell them all goodbye
And that would change the picture in your eyes
. . . then you could see the picture in His eyes

From the song "The Picture in His Eyes" on the CD *Banish the Myth.*

❦❦❦❦

CHAPTER 8

Jesus Freaks

Winter, 1976.

A young woman walked down a deserted country road in the dark.

In a dimension beyond Earth, an angel sped through celestial space at a speed exceeding light. The giant wings beat with power upon the rushing air as the form of the angel circled the earth and found itself beside a tiny pond in the Michigan countryside. The angel again took flight, searching for, and finally finding, the form of a young woman walking alone on a desolate road. The angel stood ready to give a message from the Father, a task the heavenly being cherished with all of his unfallen heart.

But just as the angel began to speak, an ugly, dark angel with a twisted face shot up out of a junk pile. A wrestling match ensued, with both angels locked in a ferocious struggle. Finally, the angel of light freed one of his mighty arms and swept the ugly, dark angel to the ground, where it remained, groveling, in a semiconscious stupor.

The holy angel spotted the woman ahead on the moonlit road, her hiking boots clopping in rhythm, her head bowed in deep thought. Heaven-born affection filled the heart of the angel, who reflected back upon the many times encounters like this one had taken place. Oh, how the angel longed to see the woman walk free in the Prince of the Host. Maybe what was needed was for this woman to hear the voice of God Himself. It was something that rarely occurred, but sometimes permission could be granted . . .

Looking wistfully toward the stars, the angel spoke with reverence,

"Oh, Great Sovereign, Holy Monarch, Your Majesty, I praise Your Name. And I request of You . . . that You, Oh King, would tell her. . ."

❦❦❦❦

The night sky in Allendale was a feast for the eyes. No large city dulled the sparkle of the stars against the blue-black expanse. I was out drinking it all in one night when I decided to take a long walk. No particular goal, no curfew, I strode the gravel roads and alfalfa fields until I found a small pond in the woods. As I approached and sat, the crickets hushed, wondering if I would threaten them somehow. When I offered no further noise, they forgot me and resumed their chirping, which soon rose to a screech louder than a ten-foot speaker. I could think of no better background music for a period of intense meditation, which lasted for what seemed like hours. Certainly God would notice me now. Hidden in the obscurity of nature, no one looking on, pushing myself beyond distraction, enduring the tedium of silent, deep breathing for hours—certainly the great energy force would read my sincerity and somehow reward me.

But as I stood to go, I was still the same lonely, confused kid that I had been when I sat down. No perceptible change had come over me. Maybe I earned some kind of cosmic kudos for these types of exercises, I thought, but that's all I'm getting out of it. I'm not becoming more spiritual or more enlightened as a result of my discipline. I am still a crazy girl who can't seem to figure out what to paint on the empty canvas of life. Oh well, I sighed, why try anymore?

Suddenly, a voice interrupted my melancholy thoughts like a hand on the shoulder. It was not audible so much as it was palpable, hitting my heart directly, bypassing my eardrum. It spoke a simple, matter-of-fact sentence that I could not resist the relief of.

"I forgive you."

Three words, but an ocean full of meaning. Someone somewhere with the power to communicate from light years away . . . forgave me. Staring up at the bejeweled sky, the words brought me comfort. Someone, according to the true meaning of the word, *for*gave—before I ever asked, before I ever even admitted I needed it—gave *before* the mercy that I could not survive without.

Some feel strongly that forgiveness is only a conditional act on God's part. But the Bible concurs with the voice that spoke that night—God forgives us before we even know we need it. This *has* to be the case because if God held anything against us, we would immediately perish. The only reason we live in an unforgiven state is because we fail to receive the gift. God maintains a stance of forgiveness toward His entire fallen creation. He said, "And when you stand praying, forgive, if you have anything against anyone . . ." (Mark 11:25, NAS). Would He require us to maintain forgiveness toward sinners if He didn't do it Himself?

God came to me that night with a cosmic compassion that was as aggressive as it was restorative. My thoughts were tipped in the direction of a God with a personhood; not an ethereal pool of energy, not an inanimate mass of spirit, but a paternal, caring, personal God who could pick me out in a crowd like a father frantically searching for His child.

❦ ❦ ❦ ❦

More and more, the party life lost its attraction for me. My roommates looked constantly for a new thrill while I pretty much holed up in my room, sometimes with a friend but often alone. My ongoing dialogue with people about their various beliefs continued, but much of the fascination was gone. And my music tastes were changing. Bob Dylan blasted his cynical sermons in my ears, Joni Mitchell whined for love gone sour, but the music my cohorts loved was sounding more and more foreign to me.

One night as the music blared, a party gathered in the farmhouse. Old Steve was there, good-looking as ever, arm-in-arm with some blond. The dancers were there, pounding out a rhythm with their ever-moving feet. Some older, strange-looking fellows were there, blown in from Chicago, anxious to talk to the young ladies. There was a huge pot of some kind of stew on the stove, on which everyone was gorging. There was laughter, there was activity, there was noise, there was color, but there was no life. As I looked on the scene I could almost sense a cloud over the people, hanging low, under which they kept their locked-in obsessions. Above the cloud line, I imagined a release that they would never know if something didn't change their direction.

Then that something walked in the front door. Slowly, as if unsure they were welcome, Butch and Brian, the boys that had sublet the house to us, entered accompanied by a girl I had never seen. In one look, I perceived that Butch and Brian had undergone some type of profound transformation. They seemed to hover above the imaginary cloud line, a clear innocence in their eyes, impervious to the spirit of evil around them. The crowds of jesters parted as they moved into the room, as if the new guests were surrounded by a force field of goodness no one could bear. As I focused upon them, I saw the reason they were being avoided. Little round buttons hung on their shirts with phrases like "Jesus Saves!" and "Praise the Lord!"—Not the kind of thing you would expect at a wild party.

Oh, no, I thought, Jesus freaks! If there was one thing that bugged me more than name-only Christians, it was Jesus freaks, who couldn't seem to respect people's boundaries! Anticipating that they would accost me any minute, I withdrew to another room, after politely telling them to help themselves to the food.

The corner offered me no peace. I knew that they would be totally ignored by everyone there, and I felt pity for them. But I knew as well that they had one item on the agenda—their religion—and I didn't want to be a Jesus freak! Suddenly I heard that same calm voice that had spoken to me a few nights ago on a country road. This time it remonstrated with me like a patient mother,

"You, Jennifer, have been open to everything this world has to offer you. You have listened eagerly to Buddhists, Jesuits, Taoists, Hindus, feminists, Jewish Mystics, occultists, spiritualists, and intellectuals. You have tried everything at least once. Shouldn't you give these people a fair hearing?"

The logic of the argument was irresistible. I said, "You know, Whoever you are, you're right!"

Walking up to the Christians as they sat cross-legged at a low "table" in our "dining room" (we were college students—nobody owned furniture) I was my direct self. "OK. You can tell me about your religion," I said.

I was deeply entrenched at this point in astrology, and my sign was Pisces, the fish. I identified with this thoroughly because I loved water, having swum avidly since I was small. And the first words these Christians spoke conjured up that very image.

"It's like water," the girl, Sherry, chirped up. "You taste the water of life, you feel it, and you want more. . . you just keep drinking . . . you never thirst again. That's what knowing Jesus is like."

Well, maybe this is worth hearing about, I thought. I sat listening to the three of them speak with animation, oblivious to the people around us. Sherry was the most talkative, with Brian coming in second, his face straining with sincerity as he spoke. Butch was quiet and pensive, but nodded in agreement to everything they said. Poor Butch, I thought. He was a beautiful-looking boy with sandy brown hair and ocean-blue eyes, but there was a certain pathos in his face—perhaps the sweet sorrow of a man who had found light through the darkness.

"We went into this church, and we heard about heaven and hell, and we learned that Jesus was the Savior, not Krishna, not Maharaji, but *Jesus*," Brian shared, "and everyone who accepts Him will be saved."

I had heard it all before. Televangelists, comic strips, my mom's born-again Christian friend, I had been exposed to the jargon and I knew the script. But somehow I could not write these serious young crusaders off as being religious parrots. This thing was *real* to them. They spoke of Jesus as if He was a presence in their lives, a true friend. I listened, trying to remain detached, but not able. Could it all be true? Could my denunciation of Christianity have been a blind thrust at the very truth I had been searching for? Could the very fabric of my thinking be woven with a fatal flaw that was now unraveling?

❦❦❦❦

The next Friday night rolled around, and I was invited to go to Kiree's house with one of the older guys from Chicago who had basically moved into our house. They were friends of a sort, but I did not relish the idea of spending time with them laughing and chattering about nothing. The guy from Chicago, named Larry, had even made a sacrilegious crack about Jesus at one point that disgusted me. I felt like coming to the defense of Christianity for one of the first times in my life. Now I wished to avoid him. As I sat at my kitchen table wearing a black leotard and blue leggings, comfortable and alone in my quaint farmhouse, enjoying the absence of my rowdy roommates, I tried to think of an excuse not to go. I felt bad about standing Kiree and Larry up, but I really didn't want to see them.

Suddenly, there was a knock at the door. I flung it open to see Brian and Sherry's smiling faces. I was sincerely happy to see them. Even then, I was struck with the change that was coming about in me, being happy to see these Christians.

"Oh, come in!" I cooed, seating them at the rickety little table, knowing I was in for another witnessing session. I didn't mind. It was just so nice to be around spiritual, happy people who cared.

The better part of an hour went by as they rehashed their beliefs. The quiet atmosphere of the house without a party going on was more conducive to my asking questions. Finally, they popped one on me.

"Would you like to accept Jesus Christ right now, Jennifer? We can pray right here at this table, and you can say goodbye to us with the assurance of salvation."

"Oh . . . uh. ." I was taken aback by the offer. "I don't. . . th. . think I'm quite ready. Not yet."

"OK, you need some time to think about it, I suppose," Brian said in a kind voice.

"Yeah, I do." I appreciated the fact that they respected my boundaries.

"Well, we will see you again sometime," Sherry said, rising to go. No small talk for them, they were on a mission. Farewells were exchanged, and they were gone with a bang of the flimsy screen door.

❦❦❦❦

In the vast creation, there swims a lonely sphere
Sinking in the cosmos like a tiny falling tear
Wracked with human anguish, drenched in senseless blood
Mushroom clouds, like fists raised at God
Who sees the pulsing of all of our distress
Sees His world convulsing in what seems a hopeless mess
He whose grace and goodness fills the air
Hears His name in cursing more than prayer

And now there's so much to do,
So little to do it with
Still, everything within me wants to banish the myth
Usher in the revelation of this infinite salvation, tell them
Who He really is
Forever, I live to banish the myth

If you want to see the Father, then look on His Son
Stumbling to Golgotha if for only one

From the song "Banish the Myth" on the CD *Banish the Myth.*

❦❦❦❦

CHAPTER 9

The Great Storm

Spring, 1976.

Sunday morning in Grand Rapids, Michigan was a lively time. The city had more churches per capita than any other city in the U.S. From sunrise into the night, cars flowed in and out of church parking lots, spilling their droves of dressed-up people into Catholic masses, Pentecostal praise parties and interdenominational Bible studies. Magnificent anthems, revival hymns, and cradle roll ditties rose into the sky, creating a pandemonium that the angels heard with wonder.

Spiraling down from the high heavens, one angel arrived wearing a gleeful expression. It was Sunday morning, and the young woman the angel had been assigned to, the woman who was quickly becoming an unknowing friend, was going to be invited to church. All through the ride in the car and the entrance into the building the angel was at her side, guiding, directing, fighting back the dark angels that hovered around. All through the service the angel sat by her side, and when the minister invited the people forward, this holy being wafted her with holy thoughts and feelings.

At that moment an ugly, dark angel with a twisted face came forward and sat like a sandbag upon her feet.

❦❦❦❦

Winter began to lose its grip on Michigan and puffs of warm air relaxed my spirit. Spring Break was coming, when I would visit mom and dad and have some time to think. I wanted to rehash what I had heard from the Christians in a private situation. I began to scheme; I would go to the Lake Michigan shore for long walks with my dog. I would clear my head as the waters lapped the shore. I would reevaluate all I had heard. I would crack this thing.

The following Sunday morning, Brian and Sherry showed up at my door, asking if I would like to go to church with them. These people were so outgoing! It was hard to resist their friendliness, in such sharp contrast to the coldness of most people. We drove around for a while and finally found a church in Grand Rapids that they felt comfortable in. Me, I didn't feel comfortable in any church, but I followed them inside.

Many of the trappings of the service were similar to the ones I took part in growing up; organ music, people reciting the Lord's Prayer, passing offering plates, etc. But there was something about the pastor's way of speaking that unsettled me. I recalled sermons from the Congregational services I grew up with being mostly abstract in content, replete with references to politics and spoken or read with near-perfect eloquence. The pastor in this church was talking more personally, about personal issues and practical applications of Bible texts, more or less shooting from the hip. Now he was calling those in attendance to take a stand for Christ by coming up to the altar.

I had heard about these "born-again" type of Christians. While I struggled to define and analyze what I was observing, a scary thought socked me in the gut.

"Try it."

What? Walk up there and embarrass myself in front of all these people? I brushed it off.

"Just try it," the thought persisted, "You'll never know unless you do."

"We will sing hymn number 324," the pastor said, arms outstretched. "As we are singing, brothers and sisters, I invite you to come forward and kneel with me in public declaration that you recognize the claims of Jesus upon your lives. He *is* your Savior. Make

Him your *personal* Savior."

Wait a minute, I thought. Look at this guy. Balding, spare tire, obviously never ate a vegetarian meal in his life. How can I subject myself to the ideas of these people who know nothing of the enlightened culture I come from? What if I . . . end up being like them?

"Just go up, and see if anything happens," the thought persisted.

People were filing by, some sniffing back tears, some silent, all kneeling at the altar. The hymn droned on. A strange force tugged at my heart. OK, I thought. I will try it. If this whole thing is a bunch of melodramatic fanfare, I will know soon enough. But if there is something to it all, maybe I can combine it with my eastern religion and come up with a new synthesis. Suddenly my feet felt like they were cemented into the floor. I decided I would wait for the last verse of the song, then I would walk to the altar.

Then the unthinkable happened. The church went silent. The people finished their prayer and after a few moments, the group began to disperse. I couldn't believe it. *They didn't sing the last verse!*

Now my thoughts turned to the opportunity gone by. I wondered if the Christian God was like that, holding out His hand, but snapping it shut to latecomers. My mind objected to this picture of God, but my emotions kept surging forth, saying, "What if it's true? Maybe God doesn't wait for slow people to make decisions." I felt fear pound in my heart, a fear that clutched at me often, but now it rolled into me like a storm front on a beach.

❦ ❦ ❦ ❦

I was unable to say much to Brian and Sherry, who invited me to their house for the day. I didn't eat much either, partly due to the brunch menu (fried eggs—I hated them and still do) but partly due to the darkness rolling around inside me. Normal words seemed cheap. The only thing that could have expressed what I felt was a gut-splitting scream. But I didn't even know what to scream.

I lingered until evening, when Brian and Sherry built a campfire and invited some of their roommates. Someone had a guitar which Sherry eventually picked up and began strumming. Unexpectedly, she began to sing in a loud, deep voice:

Hey sinner man, where you gonna run to?
Hey sinner man, where you gonna run to?
Hey sinner man, where you gonna run to on that day?

Staring into the campfire, I thought of the flames of hell. Could it be that Jesus was really coming, and that "on that day" there would be no place for sinners like me to run? Could it be that I would be cast headlong into ever-burning Hades, which I knew these Christians believed in? Now I realized their earnestness in pursuing me. They were convinced that I was headed for eternal fire!

Sherry lay the guitar aside, seemingly unaware that everyone absolutely hated her song. She probably would not have cared—this woman was on a mission. And me, I was in a quandary. Could I really believe in a God that would torture people forever in molten lava? I was a vegetarian who couldn't even bear to put a hook in the mouth of a fish. Could God subject people to endless suffering and Himself enjoy the luxuries of heaven at the same time? The idea seemed foreign to the idea of a compassionate God.

But then, what did I know about God? The thought kept haunting me that these Christians were right after all, that even though their God was despotic and harsh, He was still God. If I wished to be saved from hell, would I have to acknowledge this cruel Totalitarian, and out of craven fear submit to His way? Was reality really that crude? How could I possibly know the truth?

I took these brooding questions home with me and spent a week in deep thought. I was like a woman in labor—everything around me seemed to be inconsequential compared to the battle within. Mom was flustered as usual with my moodiness, but I was helpless to shrug off the burden that had settled upon me.

I began to pray. "God . . . Jesus, if you are real, you will hear me. Show me what the truth is about You. I want to go the right way in my life. Show me what kind of a God You are." I prayed ceaselessly on my long walks in the brisk spring air, down the roads and along the barren beach, but my entreaties seemed to evaporate with the steam of my breath. No reaction or response on the part of heaven confirmed my hope that there was a personal God listening. But I was almost unable to slump back into indifference. There was a burning question inside that would not be quenched by evasion. Was Jesus really God after all? And was God really love?

After a frustrating week at home, I resumed my brooding back at school, spending more and more time alone. I was in turmoil. Some people accept Christianity as naturally as a flower opens to the sun, but for me such a change represented a radical overhaul of my entire life and thinking. I had consciously rejected this Jesus, and not heard a word of objection from Him for years. But now He stood on the threshold of my life like a patient foreigner waiting for a "yes" from immigration. Every glance I made toward the door revealed the waiting One, and brought a renewed awareness that a decision had to be made, and very soon.

❦ ❦ ❦ ❦

One dark night while most of the collegiate world was worshipping the god of pleasure, I came face to face with the God of the universe. I don't remember what led to the moment, but I found myself in my tiny room on my knees. I did not know how or what to say to this Being whose claims upon me had eclipsed all else, but I knew it was time to make peace with Him. In the dark I choked out the only words I could say, over and over like a Wailing Wall lamentation, "Jesus, take me back to the Father."

My request was laced with conviction. Jesus was indeed the Son of God, the ladder of Jacob, dropped down from heaven to repair the irreparable gulf between God and humans. I staked my only claim to His mercy, which was my desperate need, and I was not disappointed. An unspeakable peace came over me and held my heart like the cradling arms of a mother. The great storm was over, and I was home.

❦ ❦ ❦ ❦

All that I've done, races I've won
Works of art and style
Money I've earned, pages I've turned
Swept into a pile
Someone strike a match now
Up it goes in smoke
Wisdom called it folly
It was no joke

Try as I might to make myself right
I indwelt a rut
All of my best put to the test
Amounted to "So what?"
Empty as a hand from
The pocket of the poor
I came barren-handed
To Your great store

Over and over, I receive the gift without price
Seems I just can't live without it
The righteousness of Christ

❦ ❦ ❦ ❦

CHAPTER 10

Vegetarian Christians

Spring, 1976.

A small group of people rattled down Highway 75 in an olive-colored van tinged with rust. As the vehicle sped down the road, they sang in off-key unison, voices shaking along with the bumps. They were singing for several reasons; to pass the time, to encourage themselves, to keep from arguing. They all knew that the day they were embarking upon was a stressful one, but one in which much good would be accomplished.

Meanwhile, a young woman strode along the same country road with her ever-present but unseen angel trailing along beside her. Her high soprano voice sailed with the wind, and for a moment flew into the open window of the passing van, and with the voices in the van formed a chord that would ascend to God for eternity.

> *Seek ye first the kingdom of God*
> *And His righteousness*
> *And all these things shall be added unto you*
> *Allelu, Alleluia.*

❦❦❦❦

Reminders of my past were smeared all over the Thomas Jefferson College campus. Reentering my life as a changed person was not an easy task. What's more, I knew so little about practical Christianity that I was confused almost immediately into my own brand of legalism.

Recognizing my own condition in the light of the holiness of God's law, I felt my need of a Savior. But not having any close contact with other Christians who could teach me the gospel, I didn't understand what the conditions for acceptance with God were. I knew that God wanted obedience. I also knew that He had forgiven my past sin. I concluded that God had indeed forgiven me, but now that I knew better, I was required to be perfect. One more sin, and that was *it.*

I can't even describe the stress this thinking brought to me. Seeing old friends, I froze in fear that they would attempt to engage me in our old pastimes. Determined to make my new beliefs plain to them, I took my Bible and sought them out, telling each one that Jesus was indeed the Son of God, and the Bible was His inspired Word. Most of them grew suddenly cold toward me, including a jazz guitarist friend from back home in Milwaukee named Mark. When I shared my convictions with him over the phone, he erupted into curses and hung up. My roommates responded with similar, but slow-burning anger. I tried to do kind things for them, like patching Linda's jean jacket and washing Lorna's dishes, but they still seemed to hate me. But Jesus had already warned His followers of every age that such things would happen. "If the world hates you," He said, "you know that it has hated Me before it hated you" (John 15:18, NAS).

Christine, Norman's girlfriend, had a different spirit. A naturally compassionate person, she listened to my story with interest. God's Spirit was moving upon her as she observed the change in me, which was most apparent in the dance studio. The day after my conversion I returned to class, wondering how I would approach dance now that I had become a Christian. As I sat on the sidelines, I observed the class before mine finishing up. Young men and women dressed in little more than underwear and tights leaped around the room, each trying to outdo the other. As never before, I was struck with how vain it all was. And what was the point? To impress people and self-glamorize, that was all I noticed. I was seeing the world, and now the world of dance, through a totally different pair of glasses.

Suddenly I knew that God was leading me away from a dance career. In fact, I knew that I could not even join my class for this one last day. There was no reason to. It did not fit with the person I had become. The dance leotard I wore was buried under corduroy pants and a blue ski parka, and though my classmates were beginning to shuck their street clothes in preparation for class, I could not open so much as the zipper on my jacket. I sat frozen on the floor when Christine frolicked up.

"Hi, Jennifer!" she said with a smile. But when, batting her long eyelashes, she peered into my face, the smile dropped. "What's wrong?" she asked, reeling back.

"I . . . I can't do it." I managed to whimper, "I can't dance anymore. I've become a Christian, Christine, and I just can't dance anymore. I don't even know why, I just know I can't." Tears were flowing down my cheeks as Christine hugged me like a mother.

I told my dance teacher I was pulling out of the class. It wasn't too late in the term, she said, to change classes, but she was sorry I was leaving. I could not reciprocate her feelings because I felt not one pang of regret. I was more than ready to move on.

Lifestyle changes are best when they spring from the heart. So often changes are made under the pressure of guilt, but here I was changing, not because I "had" to, but because I really *wanted* to. Realizing that dance for me had been a vain attempt to feel good about myself, and that only Christ could give me true security, I vowed to God that I would never dance for an audience again. Even the thought of dancing for my own self-glory was repulsive to me.

I saw the same reality at work in my relationships with boys around campus. Within weeks of my conversion, several young men that I had gotten to know during the past year came to see me, one after another. Suddenly I was high on their lists of girls to pursue. Why did they wait until that time? I am sure that the devil himself inspired them to come. He was losing me, and he tried in vain to drag me back into his lair through Christless relationships. But the "dating game" had lost its appeal. Even one Christian man named Bob seemed to like me. Because he was one of the only Christians I knew, I had a million questions for him. He answered, but with a weight to his stare that made me uncomfortable.

Those days were like a walk through a minefield as I sought out Christian fellowship, often with no success. But I stood firm, even without an earthly friend with whom to weather the changes. Suddenly a foreigner, I walked amidst whispers and hateful looks, or sometimes seductive leers, on a path that no one else could see. "And I will lead the blind by a way they do not know," the Lord had promised, "In paths they do not know I will guide them. I will make darkness into light before them And rugged places into plains. These are the things I will do, And I will not leave them undone" (Isaiah 42:16, NAS).

❦❦❦❦

As the days grew warmer, the land began to rainbow forth from the rich Michigan soil. Like never before, I saw the face of Jesus Christ in nature, which was an important part of my spiritual life. I tried to read the Bible, but the language was so strange, the words so archaic, and the concepts so new that I found my mind wandering as the words swam on the page. Brian, Sherry and Butch were not around anymore, so I had no one to lead me into a knowledge of the Word. But somehow in the midst of this, I was able to learn enough to sustain my experience. One passage that really jumped off the page was in the book of Revelation:

"And the Spirit and the bride say, Come. And let him that heareth say, Come. And let him that is athirst come. And whosoever will, let him take the water of life freely" (Revelation 22:17, KJV).

Being a visual person, I imagined the face of Jesus as He spoke these words, filled with kindness and acceptance. By the brush of the Spirit, a beautiful portrait of Christ was being painted in my once-dark mind. God was cleansing my imagination.

But my heart still yearned for Christian friends. I began my search for a church where I could connect with other believers. This was not easy in that I had no car, and lived in the middle of Michigan farmlands. But Grand Rapids was only about a half hour away, and it was a Bible belt city! There were more churches there per capita than any other city in the U.S., at least that's what I had heard. Certainly I could find a church to attend in Grand Rapids, if I could only get there . . .

One Sunday morning I woke up long before even the mice stirred. Looking out to the gray highway from my farmhouse window, I knew that all over the city churches were getting ready to open their doors. "God," I prayed, "If you want me to hitchhike to find a church, make a car go by right *now*!" In that moment a lone car raced by on the otherwise desolate highway. I donned the one dress I had, walked to the highway and stuck out my thumb.

Arriving in Grand Rapids, I stumbled onto a Lutheran church of a modest size. I entered the doors and took a bulletin. People seemed preoccupied, so without exchanging words with anyone, I sauntered into the sanctuary and sat down. The service went on for about an hour, and all I remember from it was the fact that not one person even looked me in the eye. It seemed these people went to this place to ignore one another in a collective setting. How strange, when what drew me to church in the first place was a desire for fellowship. Didn't these people feel the same way? Weren't they here for the purpose of sharing? Apparently not. I left that day without so much as a hello.

My traipse through Grand Rapids had been fruitless. I returned to my farmhouse no more connected than I was when I left. What a waste of time, I thought, and besides, hitchhiking is dangerous. Maybe a local church was the answer.

I took the yellow pages and looked for churches in Allendale. There weren't many, but one caught my eye, "Deeper Life Tabernacle." I liked the ring of that because that was precisely what I wanted, a *deeper life*. My fingers dialed quickly and a cheerful voice chimed over the receiver.

"Hello! Deeper Life!"

"Hi, uh, I just became a Christian and I . . . uh, want to come to a church, and . . . " I stammered.

The voice cut in, "Our morning services are over, but we have a service tonight at 7 o'clock."

"Uh, how do you get there?" I asked. The voice went on to give me directions that I recognized were within walking distance.

Maybe *this* was the church God wanted me to attend, I mused. That evening I set out walking, and before an hour was past I came upon a little building down a country road that read "Deeper Life Tabernacle" on the sign outside. It looked unassuming on the outside, but the moment I passed through the doors I received a different impression. The place was as if electrified, with a commotion coming through the doors of the sanctuary such as I had never seen in any church. On the podium was, of all things, a rock band! Fellows playing drums, bass and electric guitar as feverishly as the Rolling Stones, with a cluster of women and girls singing about as poorly as Mick Jagger. Having been raised with a very formal approach to worship, this was a shock to my senses. I sat down and tried to sing along while people all around me bellowed, waving their arms in the air and swaying to the music. The song service lasted for the better part of an hour, when the players finally sat down, exhausted, and the preacher stepped onto the platform.

He was a man nearly as wide as he was tall, and he *was* tall. His demeanor was more like a cowboy in a saloon than a dignified minister. He swaggered to the pulpit with a complacent smile and eyes at half-mast.

"Brothers and sisters, praise the Lord . . . " he began, "The Spirit of the Lord is in this place . . . "

From the congregation came a rumble of affirmation. I looked around in shock, accustomed to silence during a sermon. As he continued, this man was welcoming and even encouraging response. And he wasn't content with a rumble. He built up to a stream of exclamatory statements until the people were shouting out loud. Then he went for the coup de grace,

"When we get to heaven . . . we are going to get in our Lincoln Continentals . . ."

The people boomed "AMEN! PRAISE THE LORD!"

"And we're gonna go down those streets of gold in our Cadillacs, and we're gonna go out and get us a nice, thick, juicy sirloin *steak*!" he cried.

I couldn't believe it. Here I was, a conservation-conscious, back-to-the-land vegetarian, and this man was saying that *heaven* was a place where I would drive a gas-guzzling symbol of capitalistic greed and eat poor, innocent cows! Was this Christianity after all? Would I have to discard everything that had ever rung true and become a meat-eating materialist?

I wandered home in bewilderment. Upon coming into my farmhouse kitchen, I saw a tuna fish casserole one of my roommates had made. I tried eating some, but it tasted like sandpaper to me. I really didn't want to eat meat, did I *have* to?

❦❦❦❦

I decided to go back to the Deeper Life Tabernacle and try to get some of my questions answered. The problem was, no one there actually talked to me. Even though they were friendly, they seemed distracted and forever riding on a wave of excitement. At the end of the second service I attended, the pastor made a call for those who had never given their lives to Christ to come forward. I remembered this altar call business. Going forward was not a problem for me now; I was ready — except that at this church there was an add-on:

"Come forward, those of you who have never taken a stand for Jesus Christ," the pastor boomed, "tell the world that you are His child! Take a stand for Him! Come forward and *receive the spirit!*"

People poured to the front of the church, falling on their faces, weeping and hugging one another. Enraptured in some kind of trance, they seemed moved with powerful waves of emotion. Then I listened with wonder as the strangest phenomenon of all emerged; a rhythmic sound rolled up from the floor to the ceiling, spanning the scale from deep bass to shrill treble, pouring out of every flapping mouth in the room, filling it with imperceptible babbling like mass hysteria in a foreign language. They were *all* speaking in tongues!

And the scary part was that they expected *me* to do the same.

But for me to join in their cacophony seemed like a sham. It appeared to be a mindless catharsis that belonged in a zoo rather than a church. But I remembered the altar call I had missed in the first church I had attended, and I wondered if maybe God wasn't giving me a second chance. What could I lose if I gave it a try?

Self-consciously, I dragged my body to the front of the church where the wailing session was in full swing. Babbling was not hard to manage, as I had babbled before I ever learned to talk. Soon a weeping woman had her arms around me and the pastor was thanking God that another lost lamb had come home. I felt no particular thrill at that time, but it was nice to be accepted, and even hugged, by others. It beat going to church and being ignored.

But a week later at the grocery store, I bumped into the woman who had hugged me with such empathy when I "received the Spirit." Gone were the warm words of welcome. Her glance was cold and foreign when I tried to strike up a conversation with her, and she seemed downright put off when I mentioned Christ. Where was her zeal now? Gone with the close of the church door behind her, I realized.

Neither cold formalism nor emotionalism had proved to provide the lasting Christian fellowship I needed. Neither type of church studied the word of God deeply or had many answers to the hard questions I wanted to ask. Somewhere there had to be a group of people who studied and sought the will of God together. I knew they existed, but the question was, where?

❦ ❦ ❦ ❦

It was "Food Day" at Thomas Jefferson College-a day set aside to raise awareness of the so-called "world food shortage." (Really there is no such thing. There are just greedy people circumventing the even distribution of God's bounty.) There were booths set up all over the student lobby sponsored by every group from the Red Cross to the Animal Rights Alliance. The event was of great interest to me because my own personal research had revealed that it took seven times more land to feed a meateater than a vegetarian (*Diet for a Small Planet*, 9). But wandering around the booths I felt the same spiritual hunger that had gnawed at me for years. People needed more than physical food, I thought, they need the Bread of Life, Jesus Christ.

One booth was run by a religious group I had never heard of before. About five of them stood behind a table covered with food samples and literature. I thought they must be Quakers or Mennonites based on the fact that the women were in long, flowing dresses and the men wore suspenders. Suddenly one of their young men began to shout into the crowd, "I want to see Jesus Christ in you! And you!" he was pointing into the gathering crowd fixing upon different ones with his wild eyes. "And *you*!" he said, pointing to me.

I smiled. They are certainly Christian, I realized, and not shy about it. I hung around the table for quite a while, and being a perpetually hungry college student I ate about half of their samples-something called "oatburgers" and little flat cookies made out of "carob." Finally I saw the sign that said, "One each, please." Feeling guilty, I wandered over to a rack of small books and pamphlets, picking out one that said, *The Eight Laws of Health*. Browsing through it, I realized that these people were the first Christians I had ever heard of that had a burden for health and ecology as well as religion. The tract advocated a vegetarian diet and a simple lifestyle— things I had believed in long before becoming a Christian. I felt a stirring in the pit of my stomach. Maybe this is what I had been searching for.

A few days later, I stumbled upon a flyer that read, "Vegetarian Cooking Class." Always interested in learning more about how to prepare good foods, I planned to go, scanning the paper for the time and location of the event. Then I noticed a heart in the corner in which were the words, "Free of charge. Given in love by the *Seventh-day Adventists.*" These were the same people I had met at the Food Day! I made a note to attend their class.

❦ ❦ ❦ ❦

Sure enough, the women with long, flowing dresses and the men with suspenders were the first sight to greet me when I walked into the class. I seated myself in one of the uncomfortable fiberglass chairs, glancing around at a fairly full room. A man stood for the better part of an hour and talked about health, holding up large, obviously homemade posters. I realized from the information presented that the human body was originally designed for vegetarianism. Our flat teeth, our long bowel, mimicked that of other vegetarian animals. For the first time in my life my choice to be a vegetarian was being substantiated with scientific facts. The whole presentation was a charming mix of homespun wisdom and professional teaching. These people were not doctors, but they were so earnest in what they believed that their credibility was beyond question.

When the talk was over, the women in the long dresses brought out dish after dish of beautiful foods prepared from a dazzling array of ingredients. Being as hungry as usual, I gratefully heaped my plate with samples of everything from corn-oat waffles to tofu cheese cake. As I finished eating I watched the presenters, none of whom ate so much as a morsel, hurriedly cleaning up. Oh, if only I had the nerve to talk to them, I thought, but they seem so perfect, so holy even, so out of reach. My clumsy questions would only upset their pure thought waves and even damage their composure, I thought. But I hungered for their friendship. Would one of them, perhaps, risk speaking to me?

❦❦❦❦

When the snow paints my window with lace
When a warm, furry dog licks my face
When the wind seems to sing of His grace
I believe

When I see someone do something kind
Every rainbow or flower I find
Gives me reason to make up my mind
I believe

All the devil's temptations seem strange
All my feeling and thoughts rearrange
For Jesus lives so deep within and causes the change
The moment I believe

❦❦❦❦

CHAPTER 11

Wounded But Willing

Spring, 1976.

An ugly, dark angel with a twisted face sat on the dilapidated front porch of the farmhouse on 4th Street. Next to him sat an angel that, although dark and evil, had a certain exotic quality to the face that could almost be termed beauty. The ugly angel talked in haste, scolding the other with occasional spit coming out from between his thin, black lips.

"You have failed, you pathetic excuse for a temptress! Nothing of the old ways, the ways you once taught her so well, seem to draw her now! She's not interested in self-glory, she's off drugs, she doesn't want any boyfriends, she's not even into eating junk food anymore! She's thrown away her records, her jewelry, and most of her books . . . except for those books she gets from our enemies . . . and that . . . you know what!"

The exotic angel sat expressionless through this tongue lashing until the "you know what" was mentioned. Then her eyes lit up as an eerie smile crept across her face. "That's it!" she shouted.

The other angel jumped nervously and said, "What's 'it'?"

"That . . . Book she has!" the angel hissed, "If we can't keep her from the Book, we can use the Book itself to frighten her away from our Enemy!"

A moment elapsed as this thought was processed by the slow but brilliant brain of the ugly angel. Gradually a silent grin formed on his lips, which finally broke into a smile, exposing the shiny black gums and tongue.

Then a laugh that emerged from the depths of his belly began to explode into the air. The other angel joined in until the two of them were unable to stop.

What a brilliant plan, they agreed. Use verses of the Bible itself, wrested out of context, to frighten and torment the girl until she thought that the only peace to be found was away from the Bible, away from religion, and away from Christ . . .

❦❦❦❦

"Hi, my name is Eileen," a beaming woman said, walking in my direction, "did you enjoy our class?"

"Oh, ah . . . yeah! I mean yes! Yes, I did!" I blurted, overjoyed that one of the "holy" people had been willing to break the ice.

"Do you live here on campus?" she queried.

"Ah, well, no, I. . . go to school here, but I live in. . . in a farmhouse!" I laughed, and she laughed with me. "But I'm already a vegetarian," I said, "And a Christian, and I'm so glad to find people that are both! I. . . I think this is what I've been looking for. Who are Seventh-day Adventists, and what do they believe?"

The woman stood back with a mix of apprehension and delight. I took notice of the fact that her face was one that conveyed her every emotion, almost against her will. Thin, blond hair was plastered back in a barrette, away from her round face. Bright, milky-blue eyes twinkled with joy. A merry mouth trembled and talked rapidly, breaking often into a smile that lit the room. She was unreal, I thought, what I would expect of an angel. And she's actually talking to me!

"Seventh-day Adventists believe so many different things," she said as her face grew grave. "In our name, the "Seventh-day" refers to the Sabbath, and the "Adventist" refers to the second coming of Jesus."

Sabbath? This was a new term to me. My mind moved slower than sludge trying to grasp it. "Um, what do you mean 'Sabbath'?" I asked.

"Well, the Bible teaches that man should rest on the seventh day, which is Saturday" she explained, "not the first day, which is Sunday. So we keep the day that God commanded should be kept."

Saturday? Rest? Recollections of the Saturdays of my life flipped by. Watching cartoons while eating Captain Crunch. Sleeping in.

Long, lazy days at the beach. I had *always* rested on Saturday! It was Sunday that had stressed me out. Coming home after church, dad always made us do yard work or wash the windows. So I assumed that I was obeying the Bible in resting on the seventh day. "But what about this 'Adventist' thing?" I asked.

Eileen's eyes looked toward the floor while she gathered her thoughts. Slowly, soberly, she said,

"We believe that Jesus is coming very soon, *very* soon."

I felt fear jab my heart as I thought of the implications of such an event. I hadn't heard this idea preached before except in Sherry's "sinner man" song. My heart wasn't exactly warmed by the whole thought. Visions of people running like roaches from a fire-breathing God dashed across my imagination. What was the second coming of Jesus, and how will it affect people, I wondered. Will it come without warning? Maybe these Adventist people could share something about the second coming of Christ that would help me appreciate it.

Eileen was beckoned to help finish up the cleaning, but emerged for a moment more with a pamphlet in her hand. "Here, this will help answer some of your questions," she beamed, "We are going to be having a class at the Allendale High School next week. Try to come so that we can talk."

I agreed to meet her, and, stuffing the pamphlet in the pocket of my jeans, walked out of the building on cloud nine. I was overcome with a sense that God was leading me to a wealth of answers, hopefully some of them in my pocket.

I thought of the peculiarity of these Seventh-day Adventists. Their language alone was enough to make them stand out in a crowd. I overheard them saying things like, "My conviction," which sounded like they had served time in prison, and "What a blessing," which made me think of a Catholic priest sprinkling holy water. I knew these things had relevant meaning to them, and I aimed to learn the language as soon as I could. As I walked through the farm fields to my house, I prayed, "God, give me a 'blessing' . . . so I can know what one is." The wind picked up a little at that moment swirling the silver-green grass at my feet. Summer birds sang, and the setting sun kissed my face. That must be what a blessing is, I thought, something spontaneous and beautiful. Thank You, God!

❦❦❦❦

Soon enough my elated feelings were trashed by one of my roommates. Sitting at breakfast the next morning, Lorna sat across from me rubbing her eyes. "I dreamed about you, Jennifer," she said with an impish smile, "do you want to know what it was?"

Afraid to say Yes or No, I murmured, "OK" through a mouthful of toast.

"Well, you had this *Bible*," she said the word as if it was profanity, "you know, like the Bible you always read. It had a black cover and it was thick and . . . " she leaned toward me, slitting her eyes, "you were *eating* the Bible!" she leaned back, smiling in triumph. I wish I could say that I didn't let it bother me, but to have a friend turn on you is always hard. An eerie spirit filled the atmosphere between us.

"I'll be gone soon, and you won't have to deal with me anymore, Lorna," I said, looking out the front door at the rising sun. I knew that I had a future somewhere with people who would understand me.

❦❦❦❦

That Friday evening, I sat on the porch with the pamphlet Eileen had given me. First off, I looked for the author's name, wondering if it might have been written by one of the people at the cooking class. On the back I found a name with a man's picture advertising some kind of radio broadcast. He was so old-fashioned looking that I almost laughed out loud. Carefully greased hair rippled over the top of his head, which was framed with horn-rimmed glasses. To me he looked more like a nuclear physicist than a spiritual leader. But I was learning with these Seventh-day Adventists not to judge by appearances. They were weird, but weren't we all?

The pamphlet dealt with the seventh-day Sabbath. First, it quoted Exodus 20:8-11 from the King James Bible:

> "Remember the Sabbath day to keep it holy. Six days shalt thou labor and do all thy work: But the seventh day is

> the Sabbath of the LORD thy God: in it thou shalt not do any work, thou nor thy son, nor thy daughter, thy manservant nor thy maidservant nor thy cattle, nor thy stranger that is within thy gates: For in six days the LORD made heaven and earth, the sea, and all that in them is, and rested the seventh day: wherefore the LORD blessed the Sabbath day and hallowed it."

God had promised to cause a special blessing to fall upon the seventh day, as if there were seven glasses, all with water except one, which held fruit juice. Only one glass contained the special blessing of the juice, the pamphlet went on to read. If you wanted that blessing, you had to drink from that glass.

Well, I want that blessing, I thought. My definition of the word "blessing" was expanding in this context. It meant that the thing blessed was set aside for holy use. From now on I will keep the Sabbath holy, because God has set *that day* aside for holy use. Because the commandment was the only one of the ten that referred to God as Creator, it stood to reason that the day should be spent in His creation.

The pamphlet went on to explain why the majority of the world kept Sunday instead of Saturday. I learned that the Christian church did keep the correct day until a compromise with pagan sun worship began to take place around A.D. 130. Eventually the Saturday Sabbath was discarded and Sunday was the officially endorsed day of worship when the church became a full-fledged civil power in A.D. 321. This changing of "times and laws" was predicted in the prophecies of Daniel and Revelation (Daniel 7:25), and stemmed from the rejection of the scriptures as the sole authority in matters of religion.

Wow, I thought, this issue is bigger than just a preference. It involves sacred and secular history, and, according to the prophets, the future as well. This knowledge lifted me above the mundaneness of life and placed me in the center of a controversy that spanned the ages. I felt a calling to stand for the truth, and honor God's command to worship on His day. My mind was made up. Starting the following Saturday, I would leave my house and commune with God in nature.

❦❦❦❦

I woke up the next morning to rock music blaring. Suddenly my roommates had decided that Saturday was a good day to have Jimmy Hendrix blast the doors off the house. I had to get out. I decided to ask Christine to come along with me on a long walk through the country. Since her experience with casting out devils through quoting the Bible, she was leaning toward Christianity anyway. I gave her a call, sharing my conviction about the Sabbath with her, and she agreed to come with me and see if she could get a "blessing" as well.

To this day I can remember the unfolding of God's creation before us on that day. The colors were brighter, the smells fresher than any I could recall. At one point we stood in a green field and recited the Lord's Prayer together. A huge Clydesdale horse lumbered by. We laughed like two children at the zoo. God's seventh-day blessing was evident, and I was sold on the idea of keeping the Sabbath holy.

❦❦❦❦

But the "Adventist" part of "Seventh-day Adventist" didn't set quite so peacefully in my mind. This thought of a soon-coming Jesus still filled me with fear rather than joy. I had read in Matthew 24 of the end times: "Watch therefore: for ye know not what hour your Lord doth come . . . Therefore be ye also ready: for in such an hour as ye think not the Son of man cometh" (Matthew 24:42, 44, KJV).

Was the coming Christ like a kid brother who sprang out from behind a bush when you least expected it? Or worse yet, like an enemy air raid that set sirens to blaring while people ran to bomb shelters? What condition did a person have to be in to avoid being among the unprepared? "Then they will begin 'to say to the mountains, "Fall on us!" and to the hills, "Cover us!"'" Jesus had said (Luke 23:30, NKJ). My heart pounded as I read these and other similar words.

A certain gloom settled over me as I went through the motions of my life. Doubts constantly thrust themselves upon my mind as the guilty conviction grew: I was just too much of a sinner to be saved. There was a cesspool of shame within me so deep and murky that I would just never come clean.

Fortunately, I remembered that the Seventh-day Adventists were going to be at the Allendale High School for one of their classes that week. I thought maybe Eileen would be willing to let me share my fears. Sure enough, she stood there beaming like a lighthouse as I walked in the door. I couldn't understand how a person could be so kind, but it sure felt nice.

"Jeeeennnifer!" she cooed, as if someone of great distinction had arrived.

"Oh, Hi Eileen," I said softly.

"You seem a little less than happy," she observed, tugging me to the back of the room, "maybe we can stand off to the side here and talk."

While the class proceeded, I opened my mind to this gentle lady. "Well, Eileen . . . " I fought emotions, "I need to know, does hell really burn forever? And if it does, then how can I possibly be perfect? I think I'll be lost. I'm not good enough to be saved. I just can't seem to be perfect."

Eileen was not a theologian. She gave me no sermon on the science of salvation, or "ten steps to victory" pep talk. She didn't list off the rules of Christian behavior and admonish me to obey. She didn't even list off all the texts that refute the idea of ever-burning hell fire, although they exist.* She just looked at me, a young soul, wounded but willing, and knew that I needed to see God. To this day I can effortlessly summon up the memory of her bright face as she said three words that answered all my questions and subdued all my fears:

"Jennifer, God is *love*!"

---

* I must reject the idea of an ever-burning hell on several bases, the primary one being that it is out of harmony with the character of a loving God. Could God and His redeemed possibly enjoy heaven while the lost suffered endlessly? For further study on this vital topic, try reading Malachi 4:1-3; Psalm 37:10, 20, 38; Jude 7; 2 Peter 2:6; Revelation 20:9; Hebrews 12:29 .

❦❦❦❦

There are hands like gnarled branches on an old and tired tree
There are hands so pink and tiny that they set the spirit free
There are starving children's hands with fingers dry, and thin and curled
There are ladies' hands with diamonds that could feed all of the world
There are hands that pull the trigger, yes, hands that wield knives
There are hands that torment children, and hands that batter wives
There are hands as soft as velvet, and hands as sharp as steel
But blessed are the hands that heal

And some hands hold the gavel and try to punish crime
And some hands hold the bottle, and some beg for a dime
There are some hands signing lives away in signatures of war
There are hands that treat the wounded and hands that feed the poor
There are hands that rob the downcast, yes, hands that touch with care
There hands that clench in anger, and hands that fold in prayer
But my God's hands felt all the pain of love that hands can feel
Blessed are the hands that heal

The soft hands of a woman touched her sleeping baby's eyes
Then brushed away the straw and even shooed away the flies
The baby grew into a man with hands that worked in wood
Then found their way to flesh and bone, forever doing good
So few could stand the wordless way those hands proclaimed the truth
But they just cried the louder as the iron cut them through
If God's hands were a promise, His scars became the seal
Blessed are the hands that heal

❦❦❦❦

CHAPTER 12

Part of the Holy People

Spring, 1976.

The 4th street farmhouse was now a different place. Instead of a gathering spot for dark angels, it was a war zone for both light and dark. Though they were constantly losing ground as the young woman in the upstairs room learned more and more from the Bible, the dark angels still fought for the lost dominion of her mind.

No more could the music of the world be heard pouring from the girl's bedroom door. No more was she seen at parties of pleasure or gatherings of earthly politics. No more could she be found seeking the company of young men or the release of mood-changing substances. Often she was found praying beside her bed or taking walks in the surrounding country, picking up garbage as she went. The bright angels of heaven along with God Himself rejoiced over her with singing, while the dark angels of hell were vexed with their failure to stop her ever growing love for holiness.

One dusk, the dark angels moaned as the bright angels fairly danced to watch the girl take her record collection to the end of the driveway in a black plastic garbage bag. "Good-bye, Joni," she said, free at last.

❦❦❦❦

Did I tell you that I had gotten hooked on the music of Joni Mitchell? Music can have a strange, addictive power, especially upon young people.

I tremble at this fact, being a musician myself. I feel a weight of responsibility to lead my listeners to Christ, which Joni Mitchell never did for me.

Starting out in the seventies, Joni rode on the crest of the folk music revolution. One person said of Joni's music, "There are two kinds of people in the world: those who find Joni Mitchell depressing, and those who, already depressed, find her comforting." I think I was the already-depressed type, and I did find her comforting. It seemed that my emotions were too deep for words until she spoke them, so I followed the one who had given me a voice. But I followed like a lemming over a cliff. Her early music was actually quite wholesome, filled at times with denouncements of drug abuse and free sex. Gradually, though, her life experience was polluted with a certain cynicism, until the last album I bought had her self-depicted as a boozing, smoking, one night stand. Human goodness has a way of fading when God is not in the life.

Some time after throwing away my album collection, which included at least seven of Joni's, one of my roommates put on her own Joni Mitchell album, *Blue*, and I listened. The music that had once seemed so filled with wonder and beauty now sounded pathetic and sad.

❦ ❦ ❦ ❦

During this phase of my journey, I stood alone for Jesus amidst people who, for the most part, hated Christianity. My life was in an upheaval, and I felt the stress of it. My muscles were tied in knots, and my dance training had heightened my awareness of such tensions. I could feel the current stress in my shoulders and back, leaving me unable to sleep soundly.

One night my friend Susie, about the only one left besides Christine, was spending the night and I had given her my bed. Lying on the hard wooden floor, I finally fell asleep, only to awake in the dead of night. Beside me on the floor was a man's bare foot, as if someone was standing over me. I was still groggy from sleep, but not dreaming when I spoke; "Is that you, Jesus?"

"Yes, my child, it's Me," came a soft answer.

I did not lift my head to see Him, but lay there trusting and waiting, when I felt a soft touch upon my sore back. At once, all the tension I had carried for days drained out from me, and I fell instantly asleep.

Go ahead and tell me I'm out of my mind, but I think Jesus really did touch me that night. He knew that I had little experience and support, and almost no understanding of God's Word, and so He gave me an evidence of Himself in a way I could receive it, as He did to countless afflicted people in His earthly ministry.

❦❦❦❦

I had nothing to do. I had lost the majority of my friends, quit my dance training, thrown away my albums. Buried in my tiny room, I determined to read a book that Eileen had given me called, *Steps to Christ.* On the cover, a Clint Eastwood-like Jesus knocked on the door of the United Nations building. "Will anyone answer?" it seemed to say. I will, I thought. Cracking the book, I opened to the first chapter, "God's Love For Man," reading:

> "Nature and revelation alike testify of God's love. Our Father in heaven is the source of life, of wisdom, and of joy. Look at the wonderful and beautiful things of nature. Think of their marvelous adaptation to the needs and happiness, not only of man, but of all living creatures. The sunshine and rain, that gladden and refresh the earth, the hills and seas and plains, all speak to us of the Creator's love."

The author, a lady I had never heard of named Ellen G. White, was speaking my language. I had always loved nature—in fact I had worshipped it in a way. I had spent summers backpacking on Isle Royal in Lake Superior and canoeing through the Northern Highland Lakes in Wisconsin. I knew that nature had some kind of divine power, and here, on the first page of this book, it was all put into perspective for me. Nature was not God Himself, but God's creation, a reflection of His character. I knew this had to be a great book, and I settled in to read the whole thing in a few hours time.

As evening crept over the land, the dawn was breaking in my heart. All the weeks of fear, guilt, and hopelessness gave way to the message, streaming from simple newsprint pages, that I was secure in the love of

Jesus Christ. Dark legalism disbursed and I was revived like a victim of disease given an antidote. I knew that these Adventist people had the truth that I had been crying out for since childhood.

❦❦❦❦

I stuck out my thumb one Sunday, destined for a town called Stokesville where a small Seventh-day Adventist community was located. This was the place where the people who gave the cooking classes lived. Eileen had given me the name of the place: "Woodhollow," and I located it without trouble by asking the local people in Stokesville.

Some kind stranger took me to the entrance, and I walked down a long dirt road until I gradually found civilization. Feeling as if I had walked through a time warp, I eyed the women, all in their long dresses and buns with small children toddling alongside many of them. Nowhere could I find a sign of commercialism or excess. The people, their buildings, their vehicles, were simple if not slightly impoverished. I milled around, looking for Eileen, talking to various ones I met.

Some of the people at Woodhollow were, let's just say "different." A few would preach at me, monologue-style, until I wished I could vaporize. But I had a respect for all of these people who I knew possessed the truth, and in spite of their idiosyncrasies I considered them to be holier than me.

Finally Eileen approached, with the usual beaming smile upon her face. An iron bell was ringing, and people were pouring into the main building.

"Jennifer, won't you join us for lunch?" she invited, guiding me into the growing line. A few minutes later, we filed past several women serving brown rice and vegetables. I was amazed at how simple the food was. When we sat down to eat, I pulled out a dish I had prepared at home and brought with me to share. They were very excited about trying it. I later learned that they were undergoing financial hardship which forced them to simplify the food to the point where it was a little too sparse.

It began to occur to me that, if I was to learn the truth that I was now sure these Adventists had, I should move myself to this place in order to study their lifestyle and message. When I shared this idea with Eileen, she led me through the crowded cafeteria to a slim woman with dark hair.

"Jennifer, this is the director's wife, Linda Carlson," Eileen said, as the woman stuck out her hand toward me.

"Hi," Linda said, looking at me with serious brown eyes.

Suddenly, I felt self-conscious. She seemed almost blasé, as if I was one in a long line of people waiting to ask her for something. I felt shy.

"Um . . . " I fumbled for words, "I am interested in . . . coming here to live."

I have to admit I was hoping such a proclamation would evoke some kind of happiness or welcome in this woman's demeanor, but she remained matter-of-fact, saying, "Well, there are some rules. One of them is the dress code. Women wear dresses at all times, and they should be no more than seven inches off the floor."

I looked down at my legs. Hoping to fit in, I had put on my only skirt that morning, a tan corduroy my mom had made for me. It reached just below my knees. I really didn't have any idea how many inches off the ground it was. Grasping it and looking at Linda, I asked, "Like this?"

"Well, that's kind of short!" she said in a stadium voice.

"I don't have any other dresses or skirts," I said.

"Well, you can wear it for a while until you find something else," she said. Her voice was clear and showed no emotion except a little exasperation.* I felt a thin layer of sweat break out on my skin as I flashed back for a moment to the playground of my grade school where I listened to catty girls make fun of my clothes. How could I ever let that type of thing happen again? True to my nature, I longed to be accepted, and was willing to do whatever it took to fit in. So there's a uniform? I'll wear it, just give me time.

Certainly there was some reason they felt they had to dress that way, I thought, and I'm sure it's a good one. I knew these people had the truth, and it was only a matter of time before I would discover all the details. I hiked out to the highway and stuck out my thumb, chewing on the events of the day like a cow on cud.

❦ ❦ ❦ ❦

After hitching back to Allendale, I barreled up my front steps and nearly walked inside when I noticed a box on the porch. Opening the

* Linda has really mellowed out since that time.

box, I pulled out three long skirts, a bit musty and faded, not the fabric I would have chosen, but nevertheless the right ankle length. Upon inquiring of my roommates, I learned that someone had brought them up from the basement while cleaning and they planned to throw them away. But I would keep them, I knew, because God was even giving me the clothes to wear that I might be part of the holy people.

Tearing up the stairs to my tiny room, I decided it was time to revamp everything in my wardrobe. I noticed that the people at Woodhollow were extremely simple in their dress. The women wore no jewelry or make-up, and they all pulled their hair back in large barrettes. The colors of their clothes were subdued, some downright drab. Not that I was accustomed to decking out. I wore no make-up myself, and the amethyst necklace I had used for meditation was about my only jewelry item. One extravagance I did indulge, though, was a love for perfume. I threw six or seven bottles into a plastic bag to take to the garbage. Everything unnatural or extra had to go!

Once my wardrobe was purged, I sat back and opened another book one of the Woodhollow people had given me. It was a small book called *Prophet of Destiny*. I could tell by skimming it that it was about Ellen G. White and her writings. The author had a burden to prove that she had the "gift of prophecy."

I had no problem believing that God could speak through someone, nor did I have a problem with that someone being female. Actually, Ellen White's being a woman made the idea all the more attractive to me. Because of my involvement in feminism I distrusted anything that appeared too "patriarchal," as I called it. The fact that the Seventh-day Adventist Church had a woman leader reassured me because I assumed women in general were more respected among them. I was not anxious to be part of a church that demeaned women or circumscribed their talents in any way.

The author of the book wrote clearly and concisely, giving many texts from the Bible that showed that Ellen White met all the criteria for a true prophet. The texts that impressed me the most were found in John 16:13, 14:

> "Howbeit when he, the Spirit of truth, is come, he will guide you into all truth: for he shall not speak of himself; but

whatsoever he shall hear, that shall he speak: and he will shew you things to come. He shall glorify me: for he shall receive of mine, and shall shew it unto you" (KJV).

This text clearly said that the Holy Spirit would not "glorify" Himself, but Jesus Christ. This was definitely true of how the Holy Spirit worked through Ellen White. *Steps to Christ* had filled my mind's eye with a portrait of Jesus. I have to get more of her books, I thought. I will go back to Woodhollow for a weekend, and learn all I can from these people. Picking up the phone, I dialed a number Eileen had given me.

"Woodhollow," a tired sounding voice answered. I recognized it as Billy Foster, a young man with dark hair and a stocky build. I had met him in the cafeteria.

"Oh, Hi!" I sang, "Um, this is Jennifer . . . I don't know if you remember me," I giggled.

Nothing.

"Hello?" I said into silence.

"I'm here," Billy's voice droned, "what can I do for you?"

My spirits were dampened. Obviously Billy didn't remember me. I must have made a real impression on him. "Oh, well, I just wanted to know if I could come for a visit . . . this weekend. I would just need a place to sleep. Someone told me you allow people to come and . . ."

"Just a minute," he said. A hand was cupped over the phone for several long seconds.

"OK, you can come," Billy came back, still not acknowledging me.

Wow, I thought. Eileen is always so happy to hear from me, so welcoming, and this man seemed so indifferent. Oh well, maybe Billy was having a rough day.

"Oh, thanks. I'll . . . see you later!" I said, hanging up. One thing was for sure—if I wanted to learn the truth, no one was going to spoon feed it to me. But that was fine. I had looked wistfully into heaven long enough, hoping that someday I would find the answer. God Himself, not any person, was leading me, and I would follow in His steps even if I had to walk through a brick wall.

4—T.S.

❦❦❦❦

Books of revelation prophets gave our day
Eyes ablaze with vision that took their breath away
Hungry for this knowledge, many seek in vain
Sorcerers and psychics, when God has made it plain

King of endless glory walked into our shoes
Wore our tattered uniform and paid our endless dues
Came to fight from heaven, now He takes His place
To fight the Armegeddon that all of us must face

Kingdoms fall
Michael shall stand
One for all
God as man
The revelation unfolds, the vision is clear
Michael, Michael drawing near

❦❦❦❦

CHAPTER 13

Get Ready!

Spring, 1976.

The wind raced down Highway 42 like a siren through silence. A young woman walked along the gravel with her thumb in the air. Each passing semi threw her long hair and dress into a tailspin, but after each she recovered, smiled and stuck her thumb out again as if nothing could daunt her.

A powerful angel stood behind her, walking backwards as well, with an unfelt hand on her shoulder. At one point, a rusty car passed. A twisted-looking dark angel sat in the front seat next to the driver, a tattooed man with a cigarette hanging from his lower lip.

"Oh, look at this little missy!" said the dark angel to the man. "What are you waiting for? Pick her up!"

But just as the tattooed arm began to turn the wheel, the dark angel spotted the noble bearing of the heavenly angel that excelled in strength, standing with his charge. "Oh, no!" cried the twisted angel.

"Ah, no. . ." said the tattooed man.

The rusty car sped down the highway, leaving the smiling woman to find another ride.

❦❦❦❦

The week dragged by as I waited for my trip to Woodhollow. My heart felt as if it had already moved there while my body went through the everyday machinations of school back in Allendale. Finally Friday arrived, when I threw my long skirts in a backpack and hiked out to the highway. Either because of stupidity or courage, or a mixture of both, I had no fear whatsoever of hitchhiking. Drivers were willing and helpful, and I arrived at the commune as the setting sun flickered through the oak trees.

People were gathering in "Hope Hall," the large building that held the cafeteria. An iron bell was clanging and men, women, and children were flocking to the building from all directions. Clothes were clean and pressed and some hair was still shiny-wet. Faces seemed more peaceful and many were even glowingly happy. Eileen approached with her two daughters, slender little girls with huge blue-green eyes and prairie dresses. Several young women about my age flocked together in the same flower-print frocks looking like they'd just stepped off a covered wagon.

Eileen invited me into the hall where folding chairs in neat little rows had replaced the tables and a small wooden pulpit stood empty in their midst. I sat next to Eileen and her daughters and watched with wide eyes as the people continued to pour in. Finally a very tall, elegant looking man strode to the pulpit. Adjusting a pair of glasses that glared in the low lights of the hall, he picked up a small book.

"Julia, would you please play for us, number 198, " he said in a low voice.

A lovely young woman glided to the old piano in the corner. She wore a perfectly fitted dress covered with small pink flowers that she gracefully whisked out of the way as she sat. Her perfect little head was crowned with a bun the color of honey, which bobbed like a tennis ball as she moved.

"That's Jay Wilson," Eileen whispered reverently, as if she was talking about a head of state, "and his daughter, Julia."

I looked at Julia again, then down at my faded old skirt. My long medusa-type hair spilled over my shoulders in its usual disarray. I felt like a Haight-Ashbury hippie that had walked through a time tunnel into an English colony.

Julia's finger began to dance over the keys as hymnal pages flipped. Finally Jay Wilson's tenor voice sailed out:

"Seeking the Lost, yes kindly entreating, wanderers on the

mountains astray . . . "

Up from the little crowd came a rush of voices. A profound energy filled the room as if angels were now pouring in the doors, singing and flapping their wings in time. Vocal harmony vibrated every organ of my body as I struggled to sing this song I had never heard. I had been in churches and choirs, but I had never heard a hymn sung with this kind of gusto. Finally on the third verse, I was able to pick up the tune, and in spite of myself I sang in the most powerful soprano I was capable of, adding little lilts and trills when I could find them.

Several minutes went by as one song after another was chosen and sung. Finally Julia glided back to her seat and Jay Wilson spoke again,

"Does anyone have a blessing to share with us this evening? Something the Lord has done for you this week?"

Several hands shot up from the midst of the group. Jay called on them one by one, and they stood in turn sharing stories of how God had blessed them. I was amazed at how unafraid they were to speak with candor about the Lord. They seemed honestly convinced that God was beside them every moment of every day. I was soon to learn that these illuminating little vignettes were called "testimonies."

Finally Jay strode to the pulpit and spoke again:

"Turn with me to the twelfth chapter of Revelation," he intoned as pages rustled, "verse 17. And I read, 'And the dragon was wroth with the woman, and went to make war with the remnant of her seed, which keep the commandments of God, and have the testimony of Jesus Christ' " (KJV).

Setting the Bible down, he walked to the side of the pulpit and leaned toward the people. Tearing his glasses off and wiping his forehead with his handkerchief, he said, "Do you sense that the dragon is wroth with the woman? Have you been through trials this week such as never before? Time is short my friends, and God is preparing His people for the end. Will you be ready? Will you be one of that number of which it is said, 'blessed are they that do His commandments?' "

The people whom only moments before were warbling hymns, now sat in pensive silence. Jay went on to read from Revelation 14, calling it the "three angels' message," and emphasizing the first verse,

"And I looked, and lo, a Lamb stood on mount Sion, and with him a hundred forty and four thousand, having his Father's name written in their foreheads." (KJV)

As Jay preached, I began to form a dim conception of what he was saying. Apparently Seventh-day Adventists believed that there would be two classes of people at the end of time; those that kept God's commandments, and those that didn't. The seventh-day Sabbath would then become a test of loyalty to God. Those who kept the law of God, including the correct Sabbath, would be "the saints . . . that keep the commandments of God, and the faith of Jesus" (v.12). Because of the temptations of the devil, though, many who were now part of God's commandment-keeping church would lose their resolve and fall away.

"Only those who overcome on every point will be part of that remnant," Jay finished his speech, closing his Bible, "brothers and sisters, we need to *get ready!*" The room was as quiet as a tomb.

"Shall we kneel?" Jay said, and the room began to clatter with folding chairs being thrust back as people dropped to their knees.

❦ ❦ ❦ ❦

I was shown to my lodging for the night, a sad little basement room in a house that looked as if it had been built in a hurry. I was grateful for a bed to lie in, but found it hard to sleep in a strange place. Add to that the fact that I had just heard a very scary sermon and you had one serious insomniac. I tossed in bed, wondering how in the world I could ever be part of the "remnant" when I didn't even own a flowered dress.

Like most of the people who lived at Woodhollow, I was new to the Adventist message and had a dim conception of what preparation for the end times would entail. Because we are competitive by nature, we are prone to approach the idea of the remnant as if they were some kind of spiritual elite, an exclusive club for the superrighteous. But true spiritual advancement results in a feeling of unworthiness. "The closer you come to Jesus, the more faulty you will appear in your own eyes" (*Steps to Christ,* 64). Rather than a spiritual snob society, the remnant will be a people characterized by humility and inclusiveness.

Finally morning came, with the scurrying of people upstairs. Eileen and her children lived with Eileen's brother and his wife. He was a wild-eyed fellow with pale hair and his wife was pleasant and plump. They seemed like a mismatch—he ready to come unglued at any moment, and she as predictable as canned green beans. We sat around the table eating peach crisp and bananas, making small talk.

Finally, I asked about the morning services. Were they at Hope Hall? No, a church in town. Would Jay Wilson preach again? No, there was a pastor from the "Conference," which meant the church organization, which Woodhollow was not officially a part of. The little girls sat munching quietly as I talked. Wanting to somehow engage them, I said, "So, are you looking forward to Sunday School?"

Their china-doll faces turned to me simultaneously as their voices scolded, "*Saaaaabath School!*"

I felt so dumb I almost crawled under the table. How could I have made such a stupid mistake? Seventh-day Adventists going to *Sunday* School?

❦ ❦ ❦ ❦

The church was small and white, gleaming against the spring lawn like a golf ball on a putting green. Inside it was plain, almost primitive. The un-cushioned pews were quickly lined with people, most of them from Woodhollow, and all of them plain and simple in their dress and mannerisms. Finally I spotted the pastor, who looked like he had actually styled his hair with Brill Cream, which sort of distinguished him from the rest of the group. He was a polished man with smooth ways about him, obviously a professional of a sort you would not find living in Stokesville. He strode to the pulpit and towered over the people while he addressed them. His sermon was brief, presumably because we were to have "the Lord's Supper" and a "footwashing" ceremony, which he prepared us for by reading from the letters of Paul:

> "...The Lord Jesus the same night in which he was betrayed took bread: And when he had given thanks, he brake it, and said, Take, eat: this is my body, which is broken for you:

> this do in remembrance of me. After the same manner also he took the cup, when he had supped, saying, This cup is the new testament in my blood: this do ye, as oft as ye drink it, in remembrance of me" (1 Corinthians 11:23-25 KJV).

I remembered the passage being read in church as a child, with the allusions of the bread being symbolic of the body of Jesus and the wine being symbolic of His blood. But in this little white country church the people actually broke off into groups and washed one another's feet with little white basins. This was because Jesus had commanded that the disciples should wash one another's feet (John 13:14). Afterward, they reassembled to drink thimble-sized cups of grape juice and eat some whole wheat crackers made at Woodhollow. The whole affair was a beautiful reminder of the Last Supper. I felt as if Jesus were there in our midst, quietly pointing to His cross.

Returning to Woodhollow, I was ravenous. Except for the communion bread I had just eaten, I had completely quit snacking at the advice of Eileen. The people at Woodhollow ate two meals a day and nothing in between meals except huge glasses of water. Falling into step with this program, I found that all my stomach problems had cleared up.

My previous lifestyle involved little to no breakfast, a small snack at noon and then an unending eat-a-thon beginning at about 6 P.M. and continuing until I went to bed. "You'll sleep poorly and digest poorly because you are trying to do both at the same time!" Eileen had said. Wanting to do everything right, I had immediately rearranged my habits and loved the results. But when mealtime rolled around, intense hunger created a savage urge to pig out.

I was amazed at how much the Woodhollow people ate. Willowy little children piled their plates with mountains of vegetables. Standing in the cafeteria line, I stared at the men taking six and seven pieces of bread. But they were none the chubbier for it. Suspenders were part of their uniform, but definitely not mere adornment for most of them, who were thin enough to lose their drawers without something to hold them up!

I enjoyed most of the food, except a breakfast dish made with the ubiquitous bread layered with apple sauce, baked together into a soggy mess they called "auf lauf." Under my breath I dubbed it "awful-awful."

❦❦❦❦

After lunch it was generally understood that people would take a long walk in the wooded acres that belonged to Woodhollow. As Eileen and I walked, she shared a bit of her own story with me which involved alcoholism, a failed marriage, a Christian conversion, and a miraculous change when she came to Woodhollow at her brother's bidding.

Eileen had outstripped her brother in reforming her life since she had been there, improving every opportunity to learn from the Bible and what she called "the Spirit of Prophecy." I soon understood that this phrase referred to the voluminous writings of Ellen G. White, twenty-five million words of council and instruction on everything from the end-time events to women's underwear. Eileen, like so many at Woodhollow, was determined to follow all of Ellen White's counsels to the letter.

Eileen pointed to a couple sitting on a grassy hill, and said that they were "courting." I recognized Billy Foster and a thin woman with blond hair who had served in the cafeteria. "That's Billy Foster and Meredith Cummings," said Eileen in a near whisper, "they spend time together each Sabbath, just talking and reading. They don't hold hands or touch in any way. They aren't allowed to. In a courtship, the man and woman counsel with others about whether they are suited for each other. If the brethren think that they might make a good team, they are allowed to begin their courtship. After many months of praying and spending time together, some of them decide that God is leading them to marry. I think Billy and Meredith are headed in that direction."

Finally I had found a source from which every dilemma of life could be answered. Even the complex issue of male-female relationships was made simple in this storybook land. There was black, there was white. There was right and wrong. Everything was figured out for me and all I had to do was follow the plan. Because my life had been so bereft of moral absolutes and boundaries, this kind of control was a huge, but welcome change. It was as if a weight had been lifted from my shoulders. As we traversed hills and forests, occasionally spotting other walkers in their long dresses and suspenders, I felt as if I were floating.

❦❦❦❦

"Time no longer," said the prophet
He with no beginning comes
He who started time can stop it
Can it be He waits for us?
Sing the everlasting gospel
Sound the trumpet, ring the chime
Loud with the voices of history
Perfect and plain as a rhyme
Beckoning us to keep listening
For the midnight alarm from the great clock of time

No one in the great forever
Will lament the riches lost
Or the fame he might have savored
Or the greatness of the cost
Rather for the moments wasted
He would give his one last dime
Just for a moment he squandered
Just for a chance to resign
One of the moments he wandered
As he laughed in the face of the great clock of time

He has loved us like no other
We have coldly turned away
In the person of a brother
He will come to us and say
"This is not the way I left you,
But a pious pantomime
God's broken heart is the victim,
Shutting out love is the crime
Empty religion the culprit
And you're tying the hands of the great clock of time."

❦❦❦❦

CHAPTER 14

Anorexia

Spring 1976.

Two dark angels sat on the corner of a dirt road and a highway. Over them arched the word "Woodhollow" on a hand-painted sign just big enough to be seen while speeding by on the road.

"Here she comes," said one, through a twisted mouth, "and the fun has just begun."

Both demons watched intently as a large brown station wagon rounded the corner and continued down the dirt road. The demon continued, "We haven't succeeded in keeping her from all this religion, but we can and will keep her from sharing it with anyone else."

The accompanying devil cut in, "Who are you kidding? All she does is share it! She walked all over that college campus literally reading the . . . the . . . that Book to people! Now she's telling her parents all the things she's learned. I've seen this type before. There's no shutting them down!" The devil leaned back, rubbing his hand on his head and wincing as if nursing a migraine.

The first demon sat pensively for a brief moment, finally saying, "You're right. She is almost indomitable. Almost. You see, she has things in her past we can still manipulate. We can bring her into circumstances that will make her do things that actually bring a curse upon this cause."

❦❦❦❦

With a month of school left, I knew I had to wait to at least finish the year before moving to Woodhollow. Breaking the news to my parents was not easy—but I was used to them questioning my decisions. The problem was that they had to pick me up from school and drive me—lock, stock and barrel—to this strange little cluster of people in the Michigan woods. Dad interrogated me as we packed his big station wagon.

"Woodhollow? What kind of a name is that?" he asked with a wince.

"Well, it's back in the *woods*, Dad . . . don't worry, it's the place God wants me," I assured him.

Dad was not used to hearing religious phrases come out of me, and now they were rolling off my tongue like water from a faucet. A babe in Christ, I had not yet learned tact.

"So you work there, and do they *pay* you?" he stewed.

"Well, no . . . But Jesus says 'seek ye first the kingdom of God, and all these things shall be added unto you!' " I quoted a scripture song I had learned.

"But Jennifer, don't you want to finish your *education*?" he asked.

"Yes, Dad, and Woodhollow is where I plan to do it! I will learn what I have always wanted to learn; how to cook vegetarian food, can, garden . . . all that stuff . . . not to mention studying the Word!" I said.

Dad moaned to himself, tired of my Christianness. All he had ever wanted of me was normalcy and convention. All he ever got was weirdness. Now he was carting me off to a commune where I could work for free and learn how to can tomatoes—not the kind of life he wanted for his daughter. But Dad was used to my radical ways. With a sigh he resigned himself to letting me do what I had planned, having learned so many times before that once I fastened upon a goal, there was no turning me away.

❦❦❦❦

All the thirty or so miles to Stokesville Dad and Mom were subjected to unmitigated references to God, Jesus and the Bible. I was like a child who had just learned to swim, struggling to stay above water, fearful of losing my newly acquired skill. Finally a quiet irritation settled into the atmosphere, and I realized that I was losing my audience.

But the moment we arrived at Woodhollow, they were again confronted with larger-than- life religion when a man ran up to the car.

"Prrrrrrraise God!" he cried, waving his arms, "It rained! Our crops needed rain! And the amazing thing is that it didn't rain anywhere else!"

I couldn't resist the temptation to drive the point home to my parents. "Mom, Dad . . . " I said, "did you see rain anywhere else on our way here? No! But look at the ground! Here at Woodhollow, God made it rain because they were praying for rain!"

My parents looked at the damp driveway, and then at each other without a word.

Dad turned to gaze at some of the people who were flowing in and out of Hope Hall. His brow knotted as he looked up and down at the women in their long dresses, then looked at me in mine. Finally one of the women approached and gave us instruction as to where I would be living.

"After you drop off Jennifer's things at Valleyview," she said, "you can go to Treetop . . . and have something to eat. We don't eat supper here at Woodhollow, but guests are welcome to have something light if they prefer." Valleyview . . . Treetop . . . Woodhollow . . . no evening meal! It sounded to Mom and Dad like a summer camp for the overweight.

We dropped off my things in the room where I would be living, the same basement room I had stayed in when I came for the weekend. Mom almost cried when she saw it, remembering the beautiful room I had at home. We drove like a band of mourners to Treetop where a young black girl named Phyllis showed me what was available for supper. I cheerfully set bananas, rice and peanut butter before my amazed parents, who were famished enough to choke it down, but insulted enough to eat very little.

Dad and Mom said a pensive farewell, with Dad shaking his

head and Mom fighting tears. I couldn't understand why they weren't happy! Here my life was totally straightened out, and all they could do was worry about me!

❦ ❦ ❦ ❦

A pealing bell cut through my dreams as my eyes opened wide to the near-dark. It was 6:30 A.M., and worship would begin at Hope Hall in one-half hour. Normally I woke up an hour earlier, but this morning I was late. I stumbled into my clothes and out the door with just enough time to run to the cafeteria where this daily ritual was held. Then I remembered that this was no ordinary day. Tom Carlson was scheduled to speak for the morning worship. He was the husband of Linda Carlson, the woman who had initially spoken to me about moving to Woodhollow. They had moved away shortly after I had spoken to her, to a sister institution in the south. But this week they were visiting, apparently to check up on things.

Tom was a handsome man in his early thirties, medium height and build with a pile of thick brown hair on top of his square head. There were two things that immediately struck me about him: his voice and his eyes. His voice cut the air with a tone of authority that few potentates could match, and he spoke with confidence borne of success. His face remained expressionless while he spoke, as if he might lose his edge if he showed any humanity, but his eyes smoldered with a certain warmth behind the cold front like fire through fog. They were a sapphire blue, fringed with thick lashes and heavy, almost angry brows. As he scanned the congregation gathered in the dim room that morning, he indulged in a wry smile that made him look like a monarch presiding over his subjects.

"God has given each one of us talents and gifts to use in His service," he began, "if we use them, they will grow and strengthen. If we don't use them, we will be like the servant who hid his talent in the earth (Matthew 25:14-30) . . . in outer darkness. God doesn't care how much talent you have, only how you use what you do have."

Tom talked more than preached. He seemed to connect with each person in the group individually as his eyes roved through the crowd. His message was simple, but there was a political energy that surrounded him that drove his words home. What he shared was accessible and helpful.

Little did I know that the great dichotomy that was Tom Carlson had begun to reveal itself in my life. A charismatic communicator, he could encourage people and simplify life. Unfortunately, his own wrong choices would eventually complicate his own life until it was a quagmire of sin and deceit.

❦❦❦❦

Alexis Peckham was a woman who looked a bit like a Greek statue come to life. I always considered her to be beautiful in a haunting way, with porcelain skin and large blue eyes. She was the "woman's work coordinator," which meant she was the commander-in chief of the female work force at Woodhollow. And command she did, with rigor. Alexis was tough-as-nails on the outside, but seemed plagued with a sadness that lay beneath the surface. She didn't seem to care for me, so I was surprised when she sat down next to me one day after lunch at Hope Hall.

"I noticed that you are not eating very much," she said softly, "and I'm concerned about it."

"Oh, really?" I said, surprised that she even noticed. There was a soft, motherly side to Alexis after all. And her observation was correct. I was completely delivered of my previous food addiction, and was enjoying eating very little. Too little. I was rather proud of my level of self-discipline. But now someone was expressing concern about it.

"Yes, Jennifer, you know, you need to eat in order to be strong. And there's no point in starving yourself. It won't make God love you any more," she said.

She had a point. I had heard many sermons about the need to control appetite. People at Woodhollow had no televisions, parties, fashion or money to distract them, so food was about the only earthly escape around. Many of them seemed guilt-ridden over food, publicly confessing at times to stealing food or overeating. I had picked up on this near obsession, and decided that if eating less was righteous, then eating even *less* was even more righteous.

This thinking was exacerbated by another issue that loomed large in my mind: that of the "time of trouble," which I had heard preached by Jay Wilson, and which everyone around me believed was soon to come upon the world. The Bible clearly taught that there would be such a time:

"And at that time shall Michael stand up, the great prince which standeth for the children of thy people: and there shall be a time of trouble, such as never was since there was a nation even to that same time: and at that time thy people shall be delivered, every one that shall be found written in the book" (Daniel 12:1, KJV).

This time was to be "such as never was"—something more gruesome than any war, holocaust or inquisition that had ever shaken the planet. Torture, starvation, disease and death were to be found on every side. How could I, who had grown up in a house with central heat and carpeting, ever be prepared for such hardship? I decided that I had to accustom myself to hunger in order to overcome my fear of future suffering.

❦ ❦ ❦ ❦

It wasn't until late summer when my mother visited that I realized how far things had gone. As I changed clothes and my mom sat waiting for me, she suddenly let out a shriek.

"What, Mom?" I spun around to see her eyes as wide as saucers.

"Look at you! I can see your *ribs*!" she whimpered, "You're so . . . *thin!*" Her face twisted with worry.

Blushing, I looked down at my ribs, which were easy to see, covered only with skin pulled taut like rubber gloves on a surgeon's hand. I never looked at myself, but now I saw myself through my mother's eyes. I had to admit it was a huge change from the curves I once sported. Somehow it didn't phase me, though. I liked myself small and weightless.

It would be years before I overcame anorexia. Even now, it's hard to admit I had a bad case of it. Strangely enough, the one who was finally able to help me was someone who himself once had a bad case of self-starvation.

Michael Schwirzer was the farm manager at Woodhollow; someone I rarely spoke to because women and men did not mingle, but whom I admired nevertheless. Michael worked like a horse and sang like a lark. Each morning I would wake to his sonorous tenor voice floating into my window as he walked to the fields. I was unaware of the fact that Michael was observing me, remembering his own near-death experiences with fanatical diets.

One day he walked into the health food store where I worked. He nonchalantly chose some raisins and handed them to me as I stood at the cash register. The store was tiny, and I blushed a little thinking about the fact that we were alone in a very small room. He had not said a word, but his presence was gentle, almost like an old friend.

"I noticed that you are losing weight," he said, breaking the silence, "and I'm praying for you."

Stunned, I dropped the change from his purchase into his palm and handed him the bag. This quiet, dark-haired stranger had not only spoken to me, but he had expressed concern and *was praying for me!*

"Thanks," I said in a wide-eyed whisper as he vanished through the door.

❦ ❦ ❦ ❦

I was a simple girl of Bethany
Until the day I ran away
Far from the lies of a Pharisee
Vowing I'd somehow make him pay
I tried to find a life in Magdala
But I was dying by degrees
Then came a man with the heart of God
I found myself upon my knees

I never planned it the way it went
I was just moved with sacrifice
Now that I see it in retrospect
It was a portrait of the Christ

And the call came, and my feet could run no faster
And the oil flowed, like the blood that soon would run
And my heart broke like a flask of alabaster
And the Lord said to everyone, "Tell what she's done."

From the song "Another Song About Mary" on the CD *Chance of Rain.* Copyright 1998, Jennifer Jill Schwirzer.

❦ ❦ ❦ ❦

CHAPTER 15

Psychotherapy

Summer, 1976.

The psychiatrist sat in semi-darkness behind a large oak desk, holding a pencil to his lips as he pondered something his patient had said. Behind him two angels stood. One was stately and tall, one dark and sniveling. The dark angel pointed to the patient and squawked, "She's a lunatic! A religious fanatic! Tell her she's hopeless!"

The tall, stately angel shook his noble head, "No, no. She's a confused young girl. Give her words of encouragement!"

The doctor cleared his throat. Studying the girl's face and form in a way that made her squirm, he maintained silence longer than was comfortable. Notes sprawled across his desk labeled her problem—"eating disorder," "anorexia," "religious cult." Her eyes wandered to the window as the doctor asked a few more questions, which she answered in terse, simple sentences. Finally he pulled himself upright and leaned forward slightly in the desk, his stern, black eyes boring into her.

"You have given me reason after reason for what you are doing," he said, "most of them religious. I cannot help you because you already have all the answers!" Pausing for a moment, he summoned up all the gravity he could for his final thrust. "Frankly, Jennifer, you scare me!"

❦❦❦❦

Spring bled into summer and the days ran together in what I considered a glorious ritual of eating, sleeping, working, praying and studying the Bible. I was moved to a new house where Billy and Meredith Foster, who were newly married, were "home heads." This meant that they had charge of the home and were the spiritual guardians of the people who lived there, which included about seven or eight single women and a married couple.

Not all the young women were what I would call close friends, but one named Jackie was someone I felt comfortable with. She was a bespeckled girl with dark skin and hair and the leftover marks of what had been a teenage bout with acne. She was a serious Bible student, not interested in the usual follies, like dating and fashion, that appealed to girls her age. One Sabbath morning, we decided to walk to church together, which was a long haul, so it gave us plenty of time to talk. Through Jackie, the Lord helped me understand the origins of the Seventh-day Adventist Church.

"William Miller was just a farmer," Jackie told me, "but the Lord raised him up to preach the second coming of Christ at a time when Christianity was terribly compromised with the world. There was a great revival. Miller believed that Jesus was going to come in 1844."

Autumn leaves poured out of the sky to our feet. I had read about William Miller, but having someone explain everything to me was always so much easier to understand.

"A group of people who, with Miller, believed Jesus was coming sold their farms and waited for Him to come in the spring of 1844. When He didn't come, many fell away, but some recalculated the time prophecy, and realized that the passages they had interpreted in fact pointed to the *fall* of 1844."

"And He didn't come again!" I knew that much.

"That's right. And they went through what we call the 'Great Disappointment.' But they continued to study and pray, and God came to their rescue. He showed them that they had calculated the time prophecies correctly, but they had predicted the wrong *event.* Something important was to happen in 1844, but it was not the second coming of Christ. As they studied on, God revealed to them that the event was, in fact, that Jesus moved from the first apartment of the heavenly sanctuary to the second. You know that, according to the Bible the sanctuary of the Old Testament was made like God's temple in heaven. God showed it to Moses, and it was built like the pattern" (Exodus 25:40).

"The first apartment was where sin was forgiven, right?" I asked.

"Yes, and the second apartment was where sin was cleansed, once a year, on Yom Kippur, the Day of Atonement. The sin had been put into the sanctuary all year when people brought animal sacrifices and confessed their sins. Then when Yom Kippur came, people were required to fast and pray while the cleansing took place."

"So, 1844 was the time when the cleansing of the heavenly sanctuary began . . . " I mused.

"And now we are in the time of the Day of Atonement, only it's more than a day!" Jackie said.

"That's a good thing," I said with a little tremble. The idea of the end of time still had a certain bite to it for me. Because of my incomplete understanding of the gospel, I viewed the whole matter with trepidation. How could I ever be sinless, I wondered.

"When all sin is cleansed from the sanctuary in heaven, Jesus will come again. Only no one knows the day or the hour, except God Himself." Jackie smiled. I could tell she was happy with herself for sharing such weighty things with me.

It occurred to me that this church I was so interested in joining had started off with a big *mistake.* Serious seekers for truth, wanting to do God's will, they had insufficient information to be perfect in their beliefs. But like Mary Magdalene, who anointed Jesus with precious perfume because she thought He was soon to be crowned king, Jesus looked, and still looks, at the heart. Incorrect information is not a problem with God if the heart is willing. "But the path of the righteous is like the light of dawn, That shines brighter and brighter until the full day" (Proverbs 4:18, NAS). He led His people in 1844 to a more complete understanding of the truth even as He led Mary, and as He will lead each one of us if our hearts desire it. "If any man will do his will, he shall know of the doctrine, whether it be of God, or whether I speak of myself" (John 7:17, KJV).

❦ ❦ ❦ ❦

One of the toughest things about eating, dressing, and generally living in a way that was totally different from the rest of the world was going home to visit the family. My brothers and sisters didn't know what to make of the "new me." My parents didn't relate to my new lifestyle either, and on top of that they were extremely worried about my loss of weight. On one particular visit, an old friend named Robin appeared at the door with Rick, my old boyfriend.

My heart pumped as I walked to the living room with them and offered them seats. What would they think of me? I sat on the hearth of the fireplace, feeling their eyes upon me as if I was a museum exhibit. The last time they had seen me I was a laughing party girl in blue jeans and wild golden hair. Now I was a pencil-thin saint in an ankle-length, outdated dress, my hair pulled back in a style as austere as the expression on my face.

"So, what religion are you, Mormon? Or is it Jehovah's Witness?" asked Rick incredulously.

"Neither. I'm studying to become a Seventh-day Adventist," I said, trying not to look at him too directly. Yet I felt his worried eyes on me.

"What do they believe?" Robin asked. She had been one of my best friends in high school—a lovely, tall girl with a high GPA.

"Well, they . . . *we* believe a lot of things," I said, summoning up my courage, "First of all, we believe in Jesus. That's the main focus of it all. And I believe in Jesus Christ as a personal Savior."

I knew that this would throw an even bigger chill into the conversation than was already there, and it did. Rick was a Jew by birth, and Robin not particularly religious. Neither of them was willing to sit through a sermon, especially one given by someone they used to know as a total heathen.

"So, if you're wondering what has happened to me, that's what it is. I have become a Christian," I said.

I avoided eye contact with them, fearing that somehow they could look into my soul and draw out what I feared the most—the old me. If I let down my guard for a moment, I thought, this ghost of Jennifer past would come rollicking into the room, stripped of inhibitions, and do something crazy.

Finally Rick summoned up his courage enough to ask me about

what troubled him the most. "Jennifer, you don't look healthy. Your face, ah . . . everything . . . is so thin," he scanned me head to toe.

I stiffened. "I'm healthy, though. I eat all natural foods now. No sugar, no dairy products, no refined foods. And I drink lots of water," but I defended myself without effect.

Robin shook her head, "I'm studying dietetics in college, and Jennifer . . . you know it's possible to become undernourished if you don't eat enough."

"Yeah," said Rick, "you used to be so . . . healthy."

Well, I thought, Rick would just have to forget how I "used to be," because I would never be that way again! And if I wanted to starve . . . uh, *discipline* myself with a better diet, then that's what I would do, whether he liked the end result or not!

Suddenly it dawned upon me that I was scaring these people. After a pause, I shifted gears, saying, "It's true I've been through big changes. I know I look different. I can't explain it all, but I know deep inside my soul that the Seventh-day Adventist Church teaches the truth. You guys remember how I always talked about finding 'the truth.' "

They nodded, and Rick rolled his eyes a little.

"Well, I have," I said.

Robin and Rick seemed moved, but unable to make comment. I have to wonder if I could have had more of an impact upon them if I had been more balanced myself. If only I had realized that I was conveying a harsh image of everything I believed in, from vegetarianism, to Seventh-day Adventism, to God Himself. Fearful of lapsing back into my past delinquency, I had built walls around myself like the Jews of old with their rules and regulations. The very things that I thought were keeping me safe were actually walling me off from the world God wanted me to reach. If only I had been more secure in Jesus, I would have been able to convey that security to Rick and Robin, and they would have seen the goodness of God through me.

But one of the amazing things about God is that He uses people wherever they are at. Looking back, I realize I had a firm hold upon the doctrines of Adventism, but I struggled with security in Christ. This lack of security led to some of my imbalances. There was more

I needed to know about the gospel of God's grace, but that would come in time.

❦❦❦❦

Later that week, Mom announced to me that she had arranged an appointment with a dietitian. Reluctantly, I subjected myself to blood sugar tests and dietary counseling, none of which would make much of an impact or change. Next, Mom sent me to two psychiatrists, one of which told me that he was afraid of me. (Imagine that! Afraid of a ninety-five pound girl! I found it amusing.) The other, who was a Christian counselor, gave me an opportunity to engage in a debate about the Bible.

Dr. Staab was a huge man with very little hair. Piled into a large chair behind his desk, he seemed amiable enough, and I thought I might even be able to enjoy a decent conversation with him, but somehow we ended up arguing about life after death.

"Oh, there *is* life after death!" I preached, "but only after the resurrection! The Bible teaches that people *sleep* in the grave. You remember, Jesus said that Lazarus was sleeping (John 11:11-14). Well, Lazarus had been dead four days when Jesus said that!"

"No, no, no!" Dr. Staab shook his head, "our dead relatives and loved ones are with the Lord, waiting for us to get there and share heaven with them."

"But the Bible says that 'the dead know not any thing,' " (Ecclesiates 9:5) I quoted my King James, "and that in the day we die our 'thoughts perish' " (Psalms 146:4).

Dr. Staab couldn't accept my views. As the conversation escalated into an argument, I secretly rejoiced that we had completely avoided the subject of anorexia.

"In one of the letters of Paul, he says that Jesus will come with a trumpet sound, '. . . and the dead in Christ shall rise first: Then we which are alive and remain shall be caught up together with them in the clouds to meet the Lord in the air!' " I said, thrilled that I remembered part of the verse by heart (1 Thessalonians 4:16, 17, KJV). "If dead people *rise*, then they were not in heaven, but in the earth, buried in the ground!"

The doctor seemed agitated. I'm sure if I had been open, he could have offered some kind of help, but instead our session had turned into a theological debate! Finally the hour was over, probably to the doctor's relief. So much for psychotherapy!

❦❦❦❦

Walking through God's storyland I see the work of Jesus' hand
Time and time again it heals, and something deep inside me feels
As if I was one of them, the ones that came time and again
Stumbling blind, outcast and lame, I am like them. . . we're all the same

Maybe I've not walked the path of harlots, thieves and sons of wrath
But with change of circumstance, I might, if given half a chance
Oh, how I relate to those who fell so low, but finally chose
To receive Your grace at last
My story echoes stories past

The woman who reached for the hem of your robe
The wee little man in the tree
The one on her knees with her face in her hands
The questioning old Pharisee
I can see so many versions of me

From the song "Versions of Me" from the CD *Chance of Rain.* Copyright 1998, Jennifer Jill Schwirzer.

❦❦❦❦

CHAPTER 16

Fanaticism

Winter 1976.

The air hung heavy as lead in the small living room of Woodhollow's largest house. What oxygen was not consumed by the fire in the fireplace was absorbed by the bodies that filled the floors and lined the walls and furniture. The central concern of the meeting at hand was a charge that was being brought against Billy Foster. The insular world of this religious commune had been shattered by an alleged crime that had already splattered the news of itself on prime-time television. All the residents were concerned and many of them bewildered. Most of them did not know what the accusation was, much less whether or not it was true.

An assembly of angels congregated in the room as well. Sorrow filled their faces, reflecting the sad occasion. The crowd murmured softly until the meeting began. At the center of the group sat Billy himself, who, after a few opening formalities, rose slowly to his feet. He then spoke in a slow, careful manner:

"I said for a while . . . that I had done nothing wrong. I thought that what I did was right, and others said it was right. But now I know the truth. What I did was wrong. I was wrong."

At that moment an angel broke away from the crowd and, circling through the veil of earth, traveled at the speed of light until only moments later, heaven was reached. He bore the news that a sinner had seen the error of his ways, the very best news an angel can share. Heaven rang with more joy over this one sinner who repented than over ninety-nine just people who needed no repentance.

❦❦❦❦

Christmas was a holy event at Woodhollow because Jesus had center stage. No pagan Santa Claus came there to compete with the thought of the birth of Christ. Snow buried us all into our wood-heated homes where we sang carols while stringing cranberries and popcorn for decoration.

Christmas had always triggered the pleasure center of my brain. I remembered deeply happy feelings from childhood Christmastimes—times of family togetherness and celebration. I remembered as a child staring at the wooden figurines of the creche, letting my mind reach back to that time when Jesus was born in a stable. What I recognize now as the Holy Spirit would warm my heart and testify to the truth of the virgin birth of a God-man in a city called Bethlehem. That God would condescend to take upon Himself our fallen human flesh left me awestruck, and still does (see Philippians 2:5-10- one of my favorite passages in the Bible).

Since my conversion, I had been dabbling in songwriting, happier with the results than I had ever been. This Christmas season afforded me a break from the hectic work schedule, and I was able to write a carol of my own, which I then shared with several of the girls. Soon we were all singing in four-part harmony:

Behold, behold the King of kings
Behold, behold, His choir sings
Behold, behold our Sacrifice
Has come to live and lay down His life

It was decided that we would perform the song for "special music" at the next community worship, which was doubly exciting because Tom Carlson, who was visiting Woodhollow again, was scheduled to be there. Everyone seemed anxious to impress Tom—somehow he elicited it.

When it came time to sing, we shyly scurried to the front of the hall hoping to at least bless a few people. With courage bolstered by each other, we sang freely, summoning a loud "Amen" at the close of the song.

I was a bit nervous when Tom walked up afterwards and asked, "Where is the girl who wrote that song?"

My girlfriends pushed me forward a little until I found my voice, "Uh, it's me. I wrote it," I said, wondering what I had done wrong.

"We need more songwriters," he said with aplomb, "and that was a really good song. You should keep writing. Can you sing it again?"

We assembled, cleared our throats and began to warble once more while Tom stood by with a beaming grin spread across his face. When we were finished, he basically commissioned me to continue to write songs and share them with whoever would listen.

His encouragement started a domino effect by inspiring me to perform another song, then another. The community soon began to recognize me as the resident psalmist-hymnwriter, an identity I enjoyed. I had begun to find my unique contribution.

If I could put in a nutshell what Tom's greatest gift was, I would say that it was encouragement. He knew how to discover people's gifts and then light a fire under them to use their God-given abilities. What a powerful influence he had over people!

❦ ❦ ❦ ❦

Damien Van Olsen was a young man who had been raised in a Christian home, but had strayed during his years as a high school student. Drugs came into the picture and absconded with the young man's brain power. Judging by the look on his face, he seemed to be little more than a walking vegetable. In desperation, his mother had sent him to Woodhollow, thinking that the simple country lifestyle might help his condition.

I remember Damien standing outside Hope Hall with a chunk of watermelon in his hand, mindlessly stuffing it into his mouth from time to time as he watched people walk by. His stare was blank in spite of beautiful blue eyes that at one time held intelligence. In fact, Damien was, in spite of his condition, a tragically attractive young man. But his large, overweight body and that blank stare made his presence ominous.

Damien was a terrible trial to Billy Foster, who was the men's work coordinator. Billy was required to motivate Damien to work. This was not an easy task. Although Damien was harmless, he would not lift a finger. This was not acceptable at Woodhollow, as people were required to work for their keep. According to what I eventually learned, Billy followed a philosophy in dealing with Damien that had been handed to him by certain members of the administration.

These leaders believed strongly in the adage, taken from a Proverb of the Bible, "spare the rod and spoil the child." I noticed that many parents at Woodhollow were not afraid to spank their children. But certain individuals at Woodhollow had taken the philosophy a step further. They reasoned that these same methods could be used upon unruly "children" in an administrative setting. What this boiled down to was that it was thought appropriate for adults to spank other adults.

Various quotations from the writings of Ellen White were used to support this idea, although there was, in fact, no such support in her writings at all. But just as thousands throughout the ages have abused and misconstrued the Bible, her counsel was misapplied and manipulated to serve preconceived ideas. How satisfied the devil is with all this, for it turns people away from the inspired writings themselves! What a risk God runs in entrusting those writings to us, who are so prone to twist and fashion them after our own warped thinking.

I was not aware of the details, but I heard at one point that Damien had died. A gloom settled over Woodhollow that made everyone talk in low tones and keep their eyes cast to the ground. When questions were asked, it was done timidly, as if knowing how Damien died was a private matter. But the authorities did not think it was private at all, and soon the media was alive with the most lurid details it could find.

It became apparent as a result of Damien's death, that he had been beaten black and blue with a rubber garden hose. This was in an attempt to motivate him to work.

A funeral came and went. Talk of Billy's soon-to-come trial buzzed in the air. One night as the entire community gathered in the largest home on the grounds, Billy stood up before all of us and confessed that what he had done was wrong. The air was thick. Many sniffed back tears and Billy's wife cried openly. Some whispered to others. No one hated or blamed Billy, but what had happened was shocking. Fanaticism had taken hold at Woodhollow.

This experience impacted me dramatically because Billy and his wife Meredith were my "home heads" or guardians. Meredith was a kind, quiet woman and someone I considered a friend. Although Billy tended to be more aloof, he had good qualities himself. I was forced, because of this, to face the fact that wrong ideas can take hold of sincere, even good, people. The danger of twisting and misusing the writings of inspiration is a very real one.

As an aside, many years later I met Damien's mother. When she heard that I was at Woodhollow when Damien died, she desperately wanted to talk to me. After discussing the event at some length, she said,

"I am glad that God was able to use Damien's death to help people realize the error they had fallen into. At least that much good came out of it all." *

❦ ❦ ❦ ❦

An autopsy was performed in behalf of the defense by a doctor from one of Woodhollow's associate institutions. Billy's wife told me that the cause of death was found by this woman to be pulmonary edema. Some believed that this would prove that Damien did not actually die from the beatings themselves, and that Billy would be found innocent. But the trial led to a conviction, and Billy was taken off to five years in prison.

---

*I am in touch with the people that live presently at Woodhollow. Though an almost entirely new set of people are there, they at times are confronted with the legacy that was handed to them. No doubt the stigma that remains is painful to them even though they were not responsible for it. I believe that the spirit of fanaticism has been thoroughly routed out and replaced by a healthier, more balanced approach.

Billy Foster served time in prison and from what I know recovered from the fanaticism he was once part of. Let us never forget that we all live because God is the God of second chances.

The idyllic world of Woodhollow was shattered into a million sharp little pieces. How could such a sour note sound in such a sweet song? I knew I had heard angels sing along with us as we had worshiped God. Evidently there were devils at Woodhollow, too, probably the most savvy ones that could be drafted out of hell. Because God was leading so many into a knowledge of Jesus, the devil was beside himself in seeking some way he could lead to bring reproach upon Woodhollow, upon the Seventh-day Adventist Church, and upon God Himself.

But anyone who knew the teachings of Jesus would be aware of the possibility that something like this could happen in God's church. Jesus said that the wheat and the tares would grow up together until the harvest (Matthew 13:24-30, 36-43). This refers to the true and false Christians within the church. It may also refer to true and false principles within the lives of those comprising the church.

God will "purify unto himself" a people (Titus 2:14, KJV) who will fully represent Him. But until that process is complete, the members of the body bring with them their emotional baggage, their wrong thinking, their sinful tendencies. The Bible itself is unsparing in its account of the wrongdoing of God's great men—from the temper of Moses to the adultery of David. In sharing the downfalls of these men, God gives us hope that even though we have similar weaknesses, we, like they, are captive to the promise. "Elijah was a man with a nature like ours," and look at the remarkable way in which God was able to use him (See James 5:17, 18). We must not deprive the world of our mistakes. God has redeemed so many of our failures. Isn't that part of the good news?

While I recognize that what happened was criminal and wrong, I tremble to think of what my sin and your sin has done to Christ. "Upon all rests the guilt of crucifying the Son of God" (*Desire of Ages,* 745). In the light of the cross, we cease to quantify sin. While no excuse can be made for what Billy Foster did, we can all afford to say, "there but by the grace of God go I."

❦❦❦❦

The man who had replaced Tom Carlson was rarely at Woodhollow due to the fact that he ran another operation in Wisconsin as well. After Damien's death, however, Peter Copeland began to make plans to move to the campus, no doubt because he saw a need for leadership. And we did need him. Against the somber background of melancholy at Woodhollow, Peter was like a clown with a bunch of balloons. Smiling, laughing, even throwing in an occasional joke, he had a way of getting people to relax and get real.

"Peter, I'm a little scared about going home to see my parents," I told him once just before a visit home. We were standing in a dark little hallway off the main floor of Hope Hall.

"Oh, don't be scared of your parents! They love you!" he said with a dramatic flair.

"Yeah, they do, but they get so down on my beliefs . . . and they pick on me for being so skinny," I admitted.

"Well, you are . . . a little skinny. . ." he said, apparently trying to find a body somewhere in my big, baggy dress. "You know, Jennifer, you may be one of those people who has to eat like a horse in order to gain weight!"

"OK, OK," I said, "but I'm leaving for home tomorrow!"

Peter sensed that my fear was real, and so he resorted to his favorite method of stress relief, which was laughter.

"Well, Jennifer, the Bible says that 'where sin abounds, grace does much more abound.' So you see sin bounding along," Peter mimicked a deer bounding around the room, "and then you see grace bounding along!" His face was lit up like a light bulb on top of his diminutive form. Then he bowed his head, crossing his feet casually and saying, "Let's pray."

After offering a simple prayer, Peter patted me on the back like an old buddy and skipped out of the building. As he stepped out into the Michigan winter night, I almost expected him to bellow,

"MEEEEERRRRY Christmas" and ride off in a reindeer-drawn sleigh.

❦ ❦ ❦ ❦

After I had lived for nine months at Woodhollow, a baptism was planned for all the young people who had come around the same

5—T.S.

time I did. Pastor Rhodes from the Stokesville church would be performing the ceremony, as no one at Woodhollow was an ordained pastor. The event was scheduled in a church some distance away.

The exceptional thing about this baptism was that it was not going to be a sprinkling of water on the head like the infant baptisms I had seen as a child. It was to be a "full immersion" baptism like the kind Jesus experienced at the hand of John the Baptist in the Jordan River (Matthew 3:13-17).

The symbolism was very real to me. We were to be baptized "...into Jesus Christ . . . buried with him . . . into death..." and raised up out of the water as Jesus was raised, "...in the likeness of his resurrection" (Romans 6:3-5, KJV). Through baptism I understood that I would be making a statement that my old self had died and I had come up from the grave a new person in Christ.

I also understood that I would be baptized "into one body," which was the church (see 1Corinthians 12:13,14), so baptism was also a declaration of my commitment to the Seventh-day Adventist faith community which God had led me to, and to the broader community of believers throughout the ages.

Thinking of these things, a solemn peace rested upon me. I was sure, so very sure, that God had been and was leading in my life. The thought that the God of heaven, the Holy Sovereign of the Universe, would come into my dark little life and escort me into this Shangri-La of truth filled my heart with awe. God was so big, but so concerned with the small things. Small things like me.

All through the service, an otherworldly atmosphere rested upon us. One by one we ascended the baptismal tank and were lowered into the cold waters, emerging to shouts of "Amen." Nothing would ever be the same. I was married to Jesus, and part of His church.

And so the journey into the church which I to this day believe holds the most advanced system of truth anywhere in the world, was navigated successfully. Now, navigating my way *within* the church, that was another story.

❦❦❦❦

A lasting friend is such a treasure
Though some have thought me crazy for continuing to care
But I believe that love can last forever
And I'll take hopeful lunacy
Over rational despair
Any day, anywhere
What can I lose? And so I chose
To search and seek and try and try again
To find and keep that treasure called a friend

Friend of mine, in spite of scars I believe in perfect healing
Friend of mine, in spite of numbing callouses I still have feeling
And I believe that love can weather any storm, and shine
So won't you be a friend of mine?

❦❦❦❦

CHAPTER 17

The Suitor

F*all 1978.*

A bearded young man knelt beside his sleeping bag under the spectacular stars of Montana's big sky. Nothing could be heard save the restful music of night in the wilderness. Against the backdrop of haunting loons and rushing water his prayer rose into heaven, and heaven heard. A beautiful angel stood by as if guarding the man, and because of the angelic presence a holy atmosphere filled the space where the man had laid his sleeping bag next to his red pickup truck.

"Dear Father, I love it here. Thank You for making this wonderful place. I want to pray for my Mom and Dad . . . and for Fifty . . . and for my friends at the mission in Honduras. And I want to know your will for my life. I am thirty-one now, God, and still single. Do you want me to . . . have a wife?"

The man dropped to face down on his sleeping bag, waiting in silence for his thoughts to collect. And then it came. A voice—a kind, paternal voice—rolled out of nowhere, saying,

"Go find Jennifer."

❦❦❦❦

For about three years after my time at Woodhollow, I lived and worked in Chicago with a vegetarian restaurant called "The New

Earth." There, with a core team of five other young Christians, we attempted to reach the people of the city for Christ. The restaurant struggled to keep its doors open, and eventually the courage of the staff began to waver.

I began to wonder if God wanted me somewhere else. I loved restaurant work because it allowed me to do a lot of cooking, which I loved to do, and gave me so many opportunities to witness to people, so I thought maybe another restaurant situation was what God wanted for me. But I wouldn't dare move unless I knew He was leading me.

One day a friend of mine came to Chicago with a delivery truck full of health foods from the wholesale business run out of Woodhollow. David Grossman had always been someone I trusted. He didn't know I was thinking and praying about a change, so his words that day came as a surprise:

"Jennifer, they need some people at the Health Line Restaurant in New York State. I don't know if you might consider going there . . . " David was a converted Jew with huge brown eyes that seemed to look right into your soul. Having made quite a journey himself out of the religion of his childhood home and into Christianity, he was able to identify with me in that we depended totally on God to lead us. "So pray about it," he added with a shrug, returning to his task of unloading the boxes of food and leaving me standing there in shock.

God must be working, I thought. "...before they call, I will answer..." was the promise (Isaiah 65:24, KJV). I had not said a word to anyone but God Himself.

Within a brief period it was settled that I would move to New York State and begin to work with the team running the Health Line Restaurant. I would make a stopover at Woodhollow for the weekend, where I would get a ride to New York. I was cheered by the prospect of seeing old friends at Woodhollow. Assuming the transition would be uneventful, I awaited the biggest shock of my life.

❦❦❦❦

I woke the morning after arriving to the sound of swaying trees—so refreshing after months of waking up to city traffic. After devotions I dressed and walked to Hope Hall as the big iron bell rang its familiar summons to morning worship. It was a small group because not everyone who lived at the community was required to attend worship anymore. Rules under Peter Copeland's leadership had loosened up a bit, and things were more informal and relaxed. After a short Bible study and prayer, a spontaneous discussion broke out about a business account that wouldn't pay a large amount of money.

Tom Carlson happened to be visiting, and he dominated. "The Bible tells us not to sue our own people, but it doesn't say we can't sue non-Christians. We should take these people to court!"

As Tom rambled on, I noticed that Mike Schwirzer was also there. I hadn't recognized him at first because he had grown a beard and put on about thirty pounds.

I had always referred to Michael as "the blue streak," because his blue jean-encased body was as slim as a streak of paint. "Streak" also referred to the fact that he always seemed to be moving faster than the speed of light. An intense worker, Michael had no time for small talk or play. He had always been elusive and yet interesting to me. Memories began to flash into my mind.

Like the time, shortly after I first arrived at Woodhollow, when I served Michael in the cafeteria line. The institution was struggling financially, and we were told to control portions as we dished out the food. When Michael came by, I doled the allotted amount of food onto his plate, expecting him to glide by so I could serve the next person in line. When his tray didn't move, I looked up into his face to see him staring at me. Our eyes locked, and I noticed that his seemed to be smouldering slightly with some kind of anger I could not identify.

"More," he muttered under his breath.

"What?" I asked. No one ever asked for more. Wanting more food was a sign of spiritual weakness, or so I thought. Certainly he wouldn't have the guts to ask for . . .

"More," he said it again, his chin set, his eyes staring straight into mine.

Well, OK, I thought, blopping another spoonful onto his plate. Thankfully he moved down the line. Later I thought about how the poor guy was just hungry. He had one of the most physically demanding jobs at the place, and he just wasn't getting enough food. I was proud of him for asking for more, whether it was a sign of weakness or not.

❦❦❦❦

Michael had left Woodhollow shortly after I did, so I was shocked to see him there that morning, looking so fine in his extra weight and his newly grown beard. He had been tree planting, which had built his muscles and tanned his skin. Watching him sit with his back to me, stroking his beard, I mused that he either didn't remember me or didn't care to say Hello.

The fact was that he was afraid to look at me. I didn't realize that the reason he had come to the Midwest from Montana was to search for me.

Later that day I bumped into him as I walked about visiting old friends. "Well, Hi, Brother Schwirzer," I said, using the formal address we always used at Woodhollow.

"Hi, Sister Wilson." Michael addressed me the same. "What brings you here?"

"Well, I am on my way to the Health Line Restaurant in Seabrook, New York . . . and you have been tree planting, haven't you?" I asked.

"Yes, in Montana," he said, "and it's so beautiful there. I love it."

"I've been to Montana and I agree. What brings you here?" I asked.

Michael searched for an answer, seemingly caught off guard. Finally he said something nebulous like, "seeing what God might have for me." I had no idea what was going on in his mind.

But Peter Copeland did. In private moments he drew Michael aside and teased, "Hey, Michael, did you see who is here? Jennifer Wilson! Hey, buddy, what are you waiting for! Come on! God is working!"

Peter had known for years that Michael was interested in me. He had expressed it to Peter before he had left for Montana, but out of shyness Michael avoided acting upon the idea. Then in the midst of the Montana wilderness God had spoken to him, saying simply, "Go find Jennifer."

Mike had tried to laugh it off, but one of his tree-planting buddies continued to bother him about it. This Cajun named "Fifty" actually told Michael to, "follow God's voice and 'go find Jennifer.' " Reluctantly, Michael packed up his red '72 Ford truck and headed for Chicago.

Arriving in the windy city, Michael found the restaurant. In signature fashion he burst into the dining room and boomed, "Where is Jennifer Wilson?"

One of the workers informed him that I had gone to New York. They didn't know that I was at Woodhollow for the weekend.

Michael thought, "Whew. That's such a relief. Just the devil after all, trying to get me to cross the country for a woman! She's not even here! I guess I'll visit Woodhollow for a few days since it's so close by . . . "

And then who should come into Hope Hall on Friday morning but Jennifer herself. Michael thought he had seen a ghost.

❦ ❦ ❦ ❦

Woodhollow advocated the practice of "courtship" rather than dating. Even though the term is antiquated, the principle involved in courtship is a timeless one. The idea is to avoid emotional and physical entanglement in the early stages of a romance. The couple seeks God's will in their lives, praying frequently for His guidance.

I had been so burned out on relationships when I came to Woodhollow that I didn't mind the moratorium on dating at all. I saw perfect sense in the idea of putting God before emotions in the relationship area. And I was happy as a single person, not feeling a need for a man other than Jesus in my life.

I was staying with my friend Betty for the weekend in her apartment on the top floor of Hope Hall. As I knelt beside my bed that night, I heard loud footsteps to the landing and a big male voice booming out. Betty walked to the head of the stairs and began speaking while I opened the door a crack. Peering out, I could see Michael's form at the foot of the semi-dark staircase. He was characteristically brief and to the point, saying,

"I want to talk to Jennifer Wilson."

Betty said, "Sure, Brother Schwirzer." Turning around to see me looking out the door, she sensed that privacy was needed, and disappeared behind her own door. I crept out to the top of the stairs.

"Y-yes?" I peeped.

Michael didn't waste any time. "I want to know if you would be willing to have a courtship with me. I could go back to tree planting and we could write letters while you work in New York. Then maybe we could come back here to Woodhollow sometime later if things worked out."

That was my first taste of the terse-bordering-on-abrupt way of Michael Schwirzer. No warming up to the idea, no gradual development of a relationship, just Boom! A huge question comes sailing out of the blue and lands in my lap.

Actually, part of the abruptness in the way Michael handled things was due to the extreme rigidity of Woodhollow's courtship policy. Even friendships between men and women were discouraged. Therefore, people had no way to even get to know each other as people, and often courtships were begun with almost no knowledge of the person except what could be gained second hand. This approach probably came about because many people at Woodhollow had previously lived on the loose side. There is a tendency in human nature to go to extremes . . .

I had to admit to myself that I found Michael attractive. He was an "all boy" kind of man, one who might be called "macho" in another setting. I felt he was out of my league, actually. Such a handsome fellow he was, and I such a little waif. I have come to realize that part of the anorexia problem, which I still had, stemmed from a subconscious desire to avoid being attractive to men. I tried to shrink down my femininity until I had the figure of an adolescent boy. And it worked for most men—they weren't interested in me, and life was simple. But somehow it didn't work with Michael Schwirzer.

"Um . . . I'll have to think about that . . ." I said, at which point Michael started to turn to go.

"OK," he said, and to my amazement, actually ran back down the stairs and out the back door of Hope Hall. Dumbfounded, I floated back to my room and flopped onto my bed. Arrrgh, I thought, now what?

❦ ❦ ❦ ❦

Climbing into the van Monday morning, I was happy to see that Michael would be riding with us to Cleveland where he planned to catch a plane to Maine. There he would visit his parents. At least we would have a couple of hours to talk in the van. The family we were riding with, the Moltons, knew that Michael had asked me to court him. But most of the way to Cleveland, Michael sat in the front while Mr. Molton drove and talked with him. I sat quietly in the back, feeling frustrated and wondering, " How can I answer this guy's question if I don't even know him? And how can I get to know him if I never talk to him?" Finally I started to pray, after which I dozed.

When I woke up, there was a bit of commotion. Apparently the van had broken down. I was used to this, as most of Woodhollow's vehicles were held together with velcro and duct tape. When, hours later, the van was fixed, Michael realized that he had missed his plane.

"Well, maybe the thing to do, then, is . . . drive out to New York with you, and hitchhike to Maine," Mike said. The Moltons agreed. At this point Mrs. Molton, a beautiful, quiet woman, whispered into her husband's ear, after which Mr. Molton nodded, then moved to the back of the car, freeing up the front seat.

"Hey, Mike, you drive!" Mr. Molton said. Mike agreed and climbed into the driver's seat, after which I climbed into the front passenger's seat. Finally I had a chance to actually talk to this fellow.

Most of the conversation was spiritual, which was fine with me. Michael loved God and the Bible, was a committed convert to Adventism like I was, and a vegetarian to boot. He shared parts of his spiritual journey with me, including a near-starvation experience he had before his Christian conversion while at a Macrobiotic* ashram.

"We were only allowed to eat so much," he said, "and that was all. But I didn't know that everyone else at the place was going out and bingeing on pizza and ice-cream while I was actually trying to live on the food they gave me. Pretty soon my weight dropped to one-twenty. I was scared, but I wanted to follow the program. Then

---

*The macrobiotic diet was associated with Taoism, a belief system that originated in the Orient and taught that life was a balance of two elements, yin and yang. Although the macrobiotic diet was vegetarian, it was too restrictive and if followed rigidly it could lead to illness.

one day I saw the leader of the ashram levitate off the floor . . . "

"You actually *saw* that?" I asked in amazement.

"Yeah," Mike said, "He told us all to fold our hands and point our index fingers at the ground, claiming that this would 'tap into the infinite power of the universe.' We were supposed to have our eyes closed, but I opened mine a crack. . . and he was literally floating about two feet off the ground with his legs crossed."

Chills ran up and down my spine. This guy had some pretty wild stories!

"I left after that, found an apartment, and collapsed on the floor. I was almost too weak to stand, but I couldn't eat because I had abused my body for so long . . . the pyloric sphincter in my small intestine had atrophied and I just couldn't hold food down. I thought I was going to starve to death."

"But you didn't," I said, looking at his muscular form, "what happened?"

"Well, there was this girl . . .a girl named Lynn. She used to visit the ashram from time to time, and I think she sort of cared about me." Mike didn't seem embarrassed by that at all, "She went to the place in search of me. Fortunately, they knew where I was. When she got to my apartment, I was lying on the floor, dying. She got some chicken broth and fed me that until I could sit up."

"So were you able to eat?" I asked.

"Eventually. I started working again, too, and regained my strength. I learned the hard way not to starve myself," he added, looking at me.

I squirmed a little, wondering if Michael had some kind of hidden agenda.

❦ ❦ ❦ ❦

Well, I'm no different than the rest
I lose the race, I fail the test
Alone I'd make an awful mess
Of this thing we call life
But heaven's love reached out to me
And turned defeat to victory
Placed love where there was enmity
And peace where war was rife

But even as His child I've tried
To serve Him out of selfish pride
But self and He cannot abide
Together in one skin
So take the heart you died to take
And make me what you died to make
And do it all for Jesus sake
And in His name, amen

The law, though holy, cannot save
It damns the noble and the brave
And ushers to their rightful grave
The best of humankind
But damned and broken at your feet
I found a peaceful, safe retreat
The pain was joy, the sorrow sweet
For love had changed my mind

From the song "Awesome" on the album *Songs in the Night.* Copyright 1989, Jennifer Jill Schwirzer.

❦ ❦ ❦ ❦

CHAPTER 18

Eighty-Five Pounds

W*inter 1978.*

Evil angels swarmed in the corners of the dark little house like maggots on a dead dog. Amidst sneers and snickers, they discussed the best way to destroy the one they hated. As she lay in weakness on her bed, they called in a demon with knowledge of germs. He had mutated and manipulated a virus until it was ferocious beyond anything previously known. Holding it up with his bony little arm, he snorted in triumph. "This one will really do her in!"

❦ ❦ ❦ ❦

The Health Line Restaurant crew lived in two houses in Dayville, New York. Shortly after my arrival there I was introduced to Marian Farnham, a strong-looking girl with pale skin and brown hair. Marian would be my roommate and would direct my work program as well. Living with the boss was not easy, especially with Marian, who could be a bit difficult to get along with. I definitely had to step completely out of my ivory tower. I learned eventually, though, that Marian had a very tender heart under a prickly coat, like a porcupine with a soft underbelly.

In the room I shared with Marian I had one place I could escape to—a closet. Inside it, I set up an altar on top of an upside-down apple crate that contained my Bible, my journal, a candle and some art supplies. My guitar sat off to the side, waiting for me to find a few free moments when I could visit my little sanctuary and sing one of my homemade songs.

The sheer number of people living in the houses made privacy a rare and precious thing. The room across the hall held a family, a room downstairs held a married couple, and our room held from two to four single women, depending upon who was visiting. In addition, there was a small sitting room, one bath, and a cramped kitchen. The other house was likewise overstuffed.

Michael hung around for a day or so, engaging various ones in conversation and telling wild stories. Everyone thoroughly enjoyed him.

I counseled with several people about the major decision I was attempting to make. The Proverbs said, "...in the multitude of counsellors there is safety" (Proverbs 11:14, KJV), so I went from person to person, laying the situation open to them and asking for their input.

Still, nothing seemed clear to me. Taking all the information I had gathered, I went into my prayer closet and told the Lord that I had no idea what to do. Part of my problem was that I was afraid of myself, of letting my own will choose what I wanted instead of submitting to God. I liked Michael. To me, he was a dream come true. I felt that this might be the chance of a lifetime, but I did not want it to be my own design. "Please speak to me," I said to God, "tell me what to do through your Word."

Reading through Proverbs, I found a section headed with "The Reward of Heeding Wisdom." The passage explained that when an individual heeded the wisdom of the Lord, he or she would be led in the right path. "He preserveth the way of His saints," the verse said:

> "Then shalt thou understand righteousness, and judgement, and equity; yea, every good path. When wisdom entereth into thine heart, and knowledge is pleasant unto thy soul; Discretion shall preserve thee, understanding shall keep thee" (Proverbs 2:9-11, KJV).

God began to shine light into my mind. I began to realize that, in my fear of doing my own will, I had asked God to manipulate me like a robot, dictating to me precisely what I should do. Although there are times when God may tell His people exactly what He wants of them, most of the time He leads us by causing us to use our own God-given faculties such as reason, conscience, and good common sense. God does not wish to make His people into mindless puppets that move with a plastered-on smile whenever the "Great Puppeteer" pulls a string! He wants to plant His Spirit into the hearts of human beings with a free will, causing them to *want* to do His will.

This is what this verse seemed to be saying to me. "I will put wisdom into your heart, and knowledge will be pleasant to your soul." My fears had convinced me that God's will could not bring pleasure, but this passage said that God would shed light upon my pathway, and it would actually be *pleasant*.

Bushel baskets of stress rolled off my shoulders. I pursued the idea in prayer, waiting for God to unfold His plan.

❦ ❦ ❦ ❦

A letter arrived from Michael. In it he described the trip to Maine, how he was picked up by a demon-possessed woman, and how he proceeded to witness to her. Then he shared how his visit had gone, with some details about how he had helped and ministered to his mother.

I remembered a statement from the pen of Ellen White:

> "Let the woman . . . inquire before she yields her affections, . . . Has my lover a mother? What is the stamp of character? Does he recognize his obligations to her? Is he mindful of her wishes and happiness? If he does not respect and honor his mother, will he manifest respect and love, kindness and attention, toward his wife?" (*Adventist Home* 47).

Michael's tender regard for his mother came through loud and clear. His desire to share the gospel with lost souls, even demon-possessed ones, was also abundantly clear. God was starting to reveal Michael's beauty of character to me, and I liked what I saw.

Within a month I had replied with a "Yes" to Michael's offer for a courtship. Fortunately, he decided to move to Dayville to cut wood for us for the winter. This would give Michael and me a chance to get to know one another better. I settled into what turned out to be several happy months of fellowship and ministry.

❦❦❦❦

"Jennifer, you are just too thin!" Fred Parker, the director of Health Line, scolded. He was sitting across from me during the restaurant lunch hour. "You need to eat more!"

"Well, Fred, you should talk," I said, eyeing Fred's beanpole upper body that bent over the table as he stuffed tofu salad and vegetable soup into his mouth.

"I'm thin, but Jennifer, look how much I eat! You barely eat anything . . . anything with any calories in it! And you love to cook things for everyone else. You make great food for Michael! Why don't you eat some of it?"

He was right. But for me, gaining weight was as hard as losing weight for a fat person. Although my anorexia was relatively mild, I still had the basic mind-set. Even at ninety-five pounds, I still felt fat sometimes. And I was almost five feet, six inches tall.

Some anorexics starve themselves to death, literally. Some develop the habit of forcing themselves to vomit, called bulemia. I was not into either of these things, and I prided myself on being in control of my situation. I just wanted to be thin, I reasoned, what was wrong with that? And yet I was deaf to people like Fred who begged me to change.

God was arranging circumstances to point out to me the gaping hole in my theories.

Michael knew as well as anyone that I had an eating disorder, but he did not have a word of condemnation for me. After all, he had been through it himself. "I know what Jennifer needs," he thought. "After we are married (Michael never doubted that would happen eventually), I will take Jennifer tree planting. She will be out in the fresh air, away from this city, this restaurant and this cramped little house. She can help me plant trees, and she will definitely get her appetite back."

So for Michael, it was only a matter of time before I would be healed. Satan, however, did not want to see that happen, and so he sent along a germ that nearly killed me.

❦❦❦❦

"Michael, I'm getting this sore on my leg," I shared with him one day, "it has just come out of nowhere . . . a big black, ugly sore, full of bumps."

"Jennifer, you think that your diet is so pure," Mike explained, "but really you don't have enough strength to fight anything." Like a fulfillment of prophecy, I was sick within a few days with a flu that turned my stomach inside out.

Now, I have had flus in my life, but nothing like this one. It so severely affected my digestive tract that I could not keep so much as fruit juice down for a solid week. Ten pounds rolled off me, bringing my weight down to *eighty-five pounds!* As I lay in the bathtub one day, I felt my bones against the porcelain and thought, "Now I see the purpose of body fat."

Fred arranged for a trip to Doctor Dane, a kind Seventh-day Adventist doctor who was sympathetic to vegetarianism. He calmly asked me question after question, taking my vitals and finally pulling out a sheet of paper. As he wrote, he talked,

"You need to drink eggs blended up with grape juice. It helps people who have been malnourished regain strength. Then I want you to go on a diet that consistently has eighteen hundred calories a day or more."

He handed me the list of foods, all of which sounded good to my starving body. Eating had suddenly become very appealing.

Although I had seen the folly of my ways, I still had to deal with the consequences of my actions. One of them was the hysteria of my parents. I learned about this from Fred Parker, who called on the phone the next day.

"Jennifer, your parents are beside themselves! They spoke to Dr. Dane and somehow got the impression that you weighed *sixty-seven* pounds! They are convinced that you are going to die and they want you to come home right away! I told them that you were doing better, and eating again, but they wouldn't listen."

"If I weighed sixty-seven pounds, I would be a sixty-seven pound corpse," I said, "but if God hadn't intervened, I might have been a corpse anyway." I knew I needed to call my parents, but somehow telling them that I weighed a full eighty-five pounds didn't seem like much reassurance. I was finally able to assuage my parent's worst fears, but they still looked askance at my lifestyle. I don't blame them. I had done one colossal job of making myself, and everyone I associated with, look like a fanatic.

❦ ❦ ❦ ❦

That event barely had time to blow over before the next one came careening around the corner. Michael and I decided to get married. We were in love! Believing that it was a union that heaven had blessed, we began to sketch out plans for the wedding.

I called Mom with the happy news, which went over like a lead balloon.

"You're *engaged*? I don't even really know Michael! Are you thinking straight, Jennifer? You've just recently been so . . . so *sick*! I can't agree with your decision!" Mom yelled over the phone receiver. I was bewildered.

But as I put myself in her shoes, I could see why she was alarmed. First off, when Michael decided to ask me to court him, he called my parents to ask for their blessing. He was following Ellen White's counsel in doing so, but he forgot to consider the fact that when my parents heard the word "court," all they thought of was tennis. They really didn't understand what he was talking about, or why he was asking.

"Mrs. Wilson, my name is Michael Schwirzer. I am acquainted with your daughter Jennifer, and I am interested in courting her. I want to let you know about my intentions," he had said to Mom on the phone.

"Courtship? Well . . . I guess it's fine . . . I don't really know what exactly you mean, but . . . go ahead," Mom had said, thinking, *Jennifer has been dating since grade school! Now that she is twenty-one, this fellow, Mike whatever, calls and asks if he can 'court' her? Oh, what next?*

What was next? That her daughter nearly died of malnourishment, and then that she was engaged, that's what was next. Sorry, Mom! I have put you through so much!

❦ ❦ ❦ ❦

Mom overcame her hysteria eventually and came to terms with the fact that I really wanted to marry Michael. He came out to visit them for a few weeks while we planned the wedding and painted their house. I think this did a lot to warm them up to him.

The wedding was held in my parent's backyard under a large tent. It was a simple affair, which is what I wanted. My dress was a plain white princess-style that Mom made out of linen, with no frills save a touch of lace around the sleeves. Half the wedding party were my conservative Adventist friends, and half were my parent's friends. I served a vegetarian meal that some of the guest's balked at, but ate anyway.

I knew that, in spite of our many faults, God had led Michael and me together. This was the end of my search for a mate—I did and still do believe that marriage is for life. One golden moment came when my father walked me out to the altar and a beam of sun burst through the clouds of an otherwise gray day.

After the wedding, we moved to Montana where I helped Michael plant trees. The physical challenges of this lifestyle were conducive to my overcoming the anorexia. I had already realized the folly of my eating disorder, but I had to re-train my body to eat a normal amount of food. Gradually, I began to eat and look like a healthy person. My energy level rose, and my emotional resilience was regained. Before a year passed, I was tipping the scales at 120 pounds.

❦❦❦❦

Life is complete
When I can share it with another, now
Love is so sweet
I know it's worth the pain of learning how

To love and be loved
That's what every heart yearns for
Whether we want to admit it or not
To love and be loved
Seems a foolish endeavor
Yet it's forever by everyone sought

From the song "To Love and Be Loved" on the CD *Soldier of Hearts.* Copyright 1992, Jennifer Jill Schwirzer.

❦❦❦❦

CHAPTER 19

Tied Together—Far Apart

F*all, 1980.*

John Phillip Parkman was a tall, blue-eyed taxi cab driver who lived and worked in Manhattan. It was noon and he was at his favorite part of the day—lunch at Harvest House Restaurant. He knew several of the employees, and was acquainted with their beliefs partly because his girl friend had been raised in the Adventist church. He wasn't quite ready to join their religion, but as he walked toward the restaurant, he reflected on what good people they were, and how if he ever had a chance to defend one of them, he would.

As John rounded the corner, he saw a large woman standing in the middle of a crowd, almost eclipsing someone he recognized as Jennifer, the friendly girl who worked the cash register at Harvest House. The large woman was shouting obscenities at Jennifer. John pushed himself to the front of the crowd and tried to understand what was going on.

What John could not see was the dark presence of an evil angel. With a glare of excited hatred in its eyes, the angel edged closer, his shouted words like a twisted dagger. Suddenly the large woman grabbed a pick-type comb from off the ground and thrust the points at Jennifer's face.

❦ ❦ ❦ ❦

Marriage. What can I say about it? Next to accepting Christ, it's the single most important decision a person can make in life. Along with the Sabbath, it was present in the garden of Eden, an institution blessed by God, who has put within marriage a metaphor of His own relationship to His bride, the church (Ephesians 5:31, 32). The Seventh-day Adventist Church considers part of its mission to be the restoration of relationships, including marriage (Malachi 4:6; Matthew 3:1-3; Matthew 11:11-14; Isaiah 40:3, 4).

Yet over the years I have seen so many marriages fail. I have seen my own groaning beneath the tension of the baggage both Michael and I brought into it. Like most newly married couples, we had so many hopes and dreams, but so much to learn.

One of the chief lessons, and the one we are still learning, is that of unselfishness. Most marriages begin with the hot fires of romance. But then those fires die down gradually. For many, they die out totally, leaving nothing but cold ashes—a nasty reminder of what once was. Fortunately, that doesn't have to happen if another kind of love is in the picture—God's agape love. This love is not led by emotion, and therefore it remains even when feelings die. It is based on commitment to another's happiness and salvation. I can say without hesitation that God's agape love is the reason I am still married to the same man today.

❦ ❦ ❦ ❦

One of the basic differences between Michael and I was social. I am someone who needs to be in contact with people. My dream was to work with a group ministry of some sort. Michael, on the other hand, is a more reserved person. His dream was to build me a log cabin in the woods of Montana. To him this dream seemed like utopia, but to me it sounded like prison. Why we didn't realize this basic difference and iron it out before we were married is beyond me. Like I said, we had a lot to learn.

At first our happiness together was immeasurable. Michael had a job planting trees, which required us both to work hard and live very close to nature. We bought an eighteen-foot trailer, our first home, which we considered a palace compared to where he had been living—in his Ford pickup.

One of our most memorable experiences was tree planting on top of a mountain in Libby, Montana. The beautiful Tamarack Pines, that turned yellow in the fall, surrounded our little trailer and the campsites of two other families on the mountain. Other than that, we were alone. I did everything over a fire, including baking bread and making applesauce. When temperatures dropped to freezing, one of the women brought her newborn over to keep it warm. Our eighteen-foot trailer was the most plush house in the neighborhood, and so we had many such visits. By the end of our time on that mountain, both families were converted to Christ and studying the Adventist message.

We gave vegetarian cooking and nutrition classes in every town we traveled to. I would visit the local health food store, and ask them if they wanted me to give a free class to their clientele. Numerous opportunities to share opened up and friends were made.

Many adventures opened up in that first year or so. But after a time, our marriage turned into what basically amounted to a tug of war. Michael would pull toward quiet seclusion, and win for a time. When the silence got too loud, however, I would scream, "I can't take it!" and pull hard in the other direction. We would end up in a place similar to Woodhollow, where people lived on top of one another. Then Michael would feel so claustrophobic that he would yank in his direction and we would end up in the woods again. It was a pretty wild ride.

After one of my yanks toward civilization, we ended up at the Harvest House Restaurant. This was an exciting project that ran a restaurant in New York City. The restaurant was bringing in between five hundred and six hundred customers a day. It was a busy, crazy place. Just the kind of thing I loved and Michael hated.

And one of the reasons Michael hated it was because Tom Carlson was the director. Michael had been somewhat traumatized by Damien Van Olsen's death at Woodhollow because he was present when Damien died. He felt that Tom contributed to the mentality behind the treatment Damien had received.

But other mutual friends were there, including David Grossman and others from Woodhollow. Eventually these factors won out and Michael agreed to move to Harvest House.

❦❦❦❦

The restaurant workers lived in the very same two houses Mike and I had lived in when we were working with Health Line Restaurant. New leadership had come in, the restaurant in Dayville had closed, and the one in New York City opened up. The energy and enthusiasm of the place was contagious, as was the charisma of Tom Carlson and his wife Linda. The staff increased constantly, and the houses were more overcrowded than ever.

Mike and I moved into a two-bedroom house that held about nine people. We had one bedroom, and the Carlsons and their son had one. Several single women lived on a closed-in porch, and two more lived in an attic that was accessed through a food closet in the kitchen. There were others in small outbuildings such as trailers, which brought the total count using the house's one bathroom and kitchen up to fifteen or more. It was comical to wake up in the morning and watch people come to breakfast from all over—including two girls who crawled down a ladder through the food closet.

It wasn't so comical to be in the bathroom and have the line outside yelling, "*ten, nine, eight, seven, six . . .*"

❦❦❦❦

Although song writing had been a steady part of my life for many years, it was at Harvest House that it really blossomed. The group had worship meetings in which everyone would gather around in a big circle for Bible study, prayer and singing. There were a couple of other women who played guitar and sang, and they would volunteer me to the group, saying, "Jennifer has a new song!" whereupon some of the people would start begging me to sing it.

I was not a born singer. My voice was breathy and the "break" between my low and high range was very bad. If asked to sing publicly, I would panic and my voice would become even weaker. So performing my songs was not something I felt comfortable with. Yet "sharing" them with people who would then learn them and sing them with me proved to be the perfect circumstances in which to grow my gift.

And Tom Carlson was a big part of this. He knew how to build a person's confidence and get them doing what they did best. He would ask me to make recordings of my songs for him, and then he would have me teach them to the group. Pretty soon the entire Harvest Home community was singing my songs.

But there was a down side to the whole thing. Some individuals noticed that Tom's encouragement of me spilled over into a sort of flattery bordering on grandiosity. It was true, I had a gift for song writing, but it was actually a modest one. Why did Tom make such a big deal out of it?

❦ ❦ ❦ ❦

It's a good thing I was as young as I was because the schedule was grueling. Restaurant workers were up at 4:30 A.M., loaded in the van by 5:00 A.M. The commute to the restaurant took about an hour and a half if there was no traffic. When we arrived, frenzied preparations were made for opening at 7:00 A.M. for breakfast, which at one point was written up in *Esquire* magazine, so hoards of people came. After breakfast hour, we closed down and had a group worship time, then made preparations for lunch.

When noon rolled around, all those skyscrapers—including the World Trade Towers that were only a block away—emptied themselves onto the streets. Swarms of people pushed into food establishments where stressed workers gobbled down food of every ilk—from grease-soaked hamburgers to sizzling steak. Then they would stampede back to their offices and stock exchange floors for more stressful hours of work. Fortunately, we had a little refuge for them in the restaurant, and food that actually lowered their cholesterol instead of raising it. There was scarcely a day when less than four hundred-five hundred people ate at Harvest House.

We served the food buffet style because of the sheer volume of people that came through in a short span of time. Often we would go through three thigh-high pots of soup, fifteen to twenty-three-foot long pans of entree, hundreds of slices of bread and all the salad fixings and desserts that went along with it. After the lunch hour, the serving area looked like a herd of pigs had stampeded through.

If you have never been involved in food service of that magnitude, you probably can't conceive of the pressure we were under every waking moment of most days. Add to that the calamities; such as the time the bucket of soy sauce spilled and leaked into the camera shop underneath us, or the mornings we had to sweep up the cockroaches because we had sprayed the night before.

Thieves of all sorts teemed in the streets of New York. There was the kind that snuck into the storefront and ran off with our bag of coins—about three hundred dollars worth. And there were the purse snatchers, and the occasional ones who tried to grab money out of the cash register. This could be as much as several hundred dollars because so much money came in.

One instance brought out the vigilante in Tom Carlson. He was eating in the dining room when two young men came to the register. David Grossman was next to me running another register, when suddenly I heard him shout, "Hey!"

I looked up to see a man poised to grab the money in my drawer. Tom came lumbering out of the dining room, spotted the would-be thief and his accomplice, and grabbed one of them by the collar. Then he threw that man into the other, and the two of them tumbled end-over-end down the flight of stairs that led out to the street. They rushed away, hoping to escape Tom. A few minutes later, one of them stuck his head back in the door to say a few choice words, and I noticed a stream of thick, red blood running down his face.

Another instance involved a stolen purse. As David Grossman and I were ringing up a constant stream of customers, he noticed a man and woman headed out—and noticed that the woman had two purses on her shoulder. He told me to run back to the dining room and find out if anyone's purse was missing. I asked Linda Carlson, who was in the dining room, to make the announcement. Her booming voice sailed out over the crowd,

"Is anyone missing a purse?"

Immediately a woman jumped up, gasping and looking toward us. Yes, she nodded, my purse is missing. I ran to the front of the store and nodded at David, who immediately grabbed the man in question, telling me to hold the woman until the police arrived. She was already headed out the door, so I followed her to the sidewalk, where a crowd began to gather.

Once I stood next to her, I realized she was about six feet tall. Looking almost straight up at her and assuming my most threatening posture, I yelled, "You're not going anywhere!"

She began to yell, "You are just doing this because I'm black! You hate black people! I didn't steal no purse! You just hate black people!"

I started to tremble, wondering if anyone in the gathering crowd would believe her and likewise accuse me. I saw faces of familiar customers, customers whom we were building relationships with, including my friend John Phillip, a black fellow who drove a cab. "Will this damage our friendships?" I wondered. "Will they believe her?" More and more curious people accumulated in a semicircle around us. Then the woman bent down to pick up her comb, which had dropped to the sidewalk. After picking it up, she motioned as if she was going to jam the prongs into my face.

Now the crowd erupted. No longer did I have to worry about whose side they were on. "Don't you touch her!" they yelled, "Leave her alone!" I sighed with relief, knowing they were ready to come to my defense.

Back in the restaurant, David was holding the man, who was also yelling accusations and flailing his arms. David was a small man, but stronger than he looked, and the man was not able to break free of David's grasp. Finally, the police arrived. After a few calls back to the station, they pulled up the couple's records. They had a list of alias names as long as their arms, were known to be thieves, and . . . the police let them go. We stood there dumbfounded that they could get away with what they did when we caught them in the act, but we eventually learned that New York City could not possibly manage the number of criminals that teemed her streets. In spite of this, Harvest House Restaurant earned a reputation of being tough on crime.

And a reputation for being a great vegetarian restaurant. Besides the writeup in *Esquire*, we had articles in *The Whole Life Times* and *Vegetarian Times*, television interviews and recommendations from the New York health guru, Gary Null. For a bunch of converted hippies, we were sure making a mark in the world.

❦ ❦ ❦ ❦

Not long after we came, the corporation purchased a farm in New Jersey. It had two houses; a large mansion and a small caretaker's cottage. The lot of us moved lock, stock and barrel to the farm, where Michael and I were given a small, stuffy attic apartment with a low ceiling. It was no palace—we could hardly stand up straight, except in the middle where the point of the roof was. We shared a bathroom and a kitchen with a family of seven who lived downstairs. The attic was infested with rats, the smell of which permeated the room, and as we lay in bed at night we could hear them scratching away in the walls.

And yet I was perfectly content. I spent most of my waking hours at the restaurant, and Michael spent most of his time growing organic vegetables on twelve of the two hundred and fifty acres. I loved working in the restaurant and he loved farming. We really didn't care much about where we lived.

The weekends on the farm were just as active. We held our church services right at the farm, and I was intensely involved in the music program. Literally hundreds of my songs were printed in songbooks and learned by the group. I had a children's choir, an adult choir and a small singing group. Even though the music was not polished or professional, it was filled with spirit and energy. In the truest sense, we made a joyful noise.

❦❦❦❦

One of the most significant things that occurred during that period of my life concerned my little sister, Kristin, who came to visit me. Having just graduated from Purdue College with a degree in marketing management, she was looking for a job. I offered to set up some interviews with the various stock brokers and salesmen who frequented the restaurant. My hope was that she would end up working in Manhattan, and we could see one another.

"Don't bring her out there," my Dad had said, "she'll end up joining that . . . *cult* or whatever it is Jennifer is a part of."

"Well, dear, it's too late," Mom answered him, "we already agreed to go. I'll try to keep a close watch on things . . ."

Kris had grown up bearing the brunt of my willingness to manipulate her. And at five years younger than I, there wasn't much I couldn't get her to do . . . like chewing tobacco, like sniffing snuff, etc. . . . the poor kid. When I became a Christian, I decided to use the same bossy-big-sister tactics to try to persuade her to do righteous things. It didn't work, but she did eventually become a Christian through Campus Crusade for Christ. I didn't realize it, but one of her great fears about embracing Seventh-day Adventism was that she wouldn't be able to wear makeup and jewelry. She didn't want to look like her plain-Jane older sister.

The morning she walked into the Harvest House restaurant with my mother, I hardly recognized her. Mom had paid for Kris to have a makeover as a graduation gift. Somewhere between the beauty parlor and the real world, though, something was lost. Pink and purple eye shadow, sparkly lipstick, glow-in-the-dark blush all flashed out from her face as if to say, "I am an individual! Don't try to make me like you!"

After several interviews during the week, Kris felt the need for God's guidance. She woke early and knelt by an apple tree in the front yard of the mansion on the Harvest House farm. After a few minutes of praying, she opened her eyes to see David Grossman standing there.

"Trust in the LORD with all thine heart . . . and he shall direct thy paths." David quoted Proverbs 3:5,6 from the King James Bible.

Kris felt her heart thump. "How did he know what I was praying about?" she wondered.

Later that day, Kris and I took a long walk down the winding country roads that surrounded the farm. I wasn't prepared for what she had to say,

"Jennifer, I've decided that I want to come live here at Harvest House."

I just about fainted. Never in my wildest imaginings did I think Kris would do that, but she felt the Lord calling her to seek for truth in the way I had. She believed that she would find it there with me.

Mom was devastated, mostly because she knew Dad would be devastated. And he was, oh, he was. Dad drove her to Woodhollow where she would pick up a ride to New Jersey. As he tried to bid her farewell, he broke down sobbing. Kristin was his youngest child, and probably his favorite. Now, as he viewed it, he was losing her to a fanatical religion.

For weeks after Kris's arrival, we worked together to memorize Matthew 19:29:

> "And everyone who has left houses or brothers or sisters or father or mother or children or farms for My name's sake, shall receive many times as much, and shall inherit eternal life."

❦❦❦❦

So many of my little dreams were finding their fulfillment at Harvest House. But I have to be honest in saying that, in spite of the constant excitement, Michael and I were really drifting apart. He wasn't thrilled with the idea of being there, and we basically led separate lives.

Looking back, I know I should have been more concerned for his happiness and less for my own. I was in my glory, surrounded with people, enjoying music and being creative. He, on the other hand, was yearning for more independence and space. The more I enjoyed myself, the more he hung back and wished we were somewhere else. Although our commitment to one another remained solid, we did not make a priority of our relationship. We were like two boats on the water attached by a long tow line—tied together, but far apart.

6—T.S.

❦❦❦❦

The sunlight plays on the gilded sea of glass
I'm light as air and I frolic like a lass
My wings are ivory, my house is tall and grand
And in the garden I can really hold God's hand

Familiar faces all streaked with happy tears
My children play and sing sweet songs amid the cheers
The chorus swells 'round the friend-forever King
But fades out when we all behold the strangest thing

No one knows quite what to do
Some poor soul is asking you
"What are these?" and pointing to
The only wounds in heaven

Isn't it an irony
There is not one mark on me
Ah, but on the hands that healed I see
The only wounds in heaven

From the song "The Only Wounds in Heaven" on the CD *Banish the Myth*.

❦❦❦❦

CHAPTER 20

Harassment

Spring, 1982.

A blue van barreled up West Side Highway, past the abandoned docks, past the graffiti-covered bridges into downtown Manhattan. Speeding alongside the van, beyond human sight, was a company of bright, holy angels. The pure senses of these beings were insulted by the evidences of sin that were everywhere in this foul place, yet their faces held joy.

The van cruised to a storefront that was set into two rows of skyscrapers so tall they looked like they were touching heaven. The angels reminisced about the tower of Babylon, remarking that it was, in fact, similar to these buildings. As a dozen people jumped one by one out of the van, the angels noticed several dark angels at the doorway of the storefront.

"We have plans!" shouted an ugly angel with a twisted face who was evidently the ringleader. "This place has done too much for your King! We hate it!" he spat on the sidewalk for emphasis, "Attacking it from the outside has not worked, it's true . . . but we will not cease our efforts. You may be able to preserve the safety of these people, but you can't choose for them. If we can lead even one to sell his soul to the Majesty of Darkness, our beloved leader, then we can corrupt it from the inside! Within five years it will come to nothing!"

❦❦❦❦

A female friend led me into her room one evening.

" I need to tell you something," she whispered, drawing out a copy of *Prophets and Kings* by Ellen G. White. She began to read about Solomon, David's son and King of Israel.

> "So gradual was Solomon's apostasy that before he was aware of it, he had wandered far from God. Almost imperceptibly he began to trust less and less in divine guidance and blessing, and to put confidence in his own strength" (*Prophets and Kings,* 55).

The account went on to report Solomon's idolatry and sexual immorality. It detailed the process by which a gradual compromise was made. Finally Solomon, once a powerful tool in God's hands, became a great influence for evil in the world.

So where is she going with all this? I wondered as she read. Finally I got my answer.

Closing the book, she said, "It's just like Tom."

"Tom? Tom Carlson?" I asked.

She looked a little annoyed. "Yes," she said, "he's following the same road as Solomon. God has given him tremendous success. He is prospering beyond all expectations. No one has ever succeeded in planting a restaurant in New York City. Tom came in and slew Goliath! Now he's known by Adventists all over the world as a sort of hero. But it's gone to his head. He's lost his connection with God. He's . . . not faithful to God." She shook her head, her eyes cast to the floor.

My mind was slow to grasp what I was hearing. After a long pause, I asked, "How do you know that?"

My friend seemed even more impatient. "I know because of . . . things he's done."

"Like what?" I asked, feeling naive.

"Like controlling people with guilt and condemnation. . . then flattery. After several years of that kind of thing, you're like putty in his hands. He knows just how to manipulate you. He's a genius! Pretty soon you're his little puppet. . ." she whispered. There was another long pause.

"So why are you telling me this?" I asked, trying to piece it all together.

"Because you're next," she said with a stare.

I really didn't fully understand what she was telling me. Apparently Tom had a manipulative streak. It was hard for me to conceive of such a thing. I wanted to believe that Harvest House was a happy family, and that all the people there were serving the Lord with all their hearts. I wanted to believe that Tom was a true Christian. I looked up to him like an older brother. As I slowly mounted the stairs back to my room, I came to the conclusion that Tom and this woman had a falling out, and she was blaming him. I just couldn't believe what she was telling me.

But Tom's behavior toward me did seem strange at times. As we sat in a circle during Bible studies, I could feel the weight of his eyes upon me. At times, he would give me special privileges or hold me up as an example. I felt like the teacher's pet, half enjoying it, and half not wanting to be because there were obvious feelings of disgust on the part of people who noticed that I was the center of attention.

When faced with these things, I would quickly reason that there was no way Tom could be attracted to me. If he was going to flirt with someone, why not one of the gorgeous Manhattan women who came into the restaurant every day? But my reasoning was out of naiveté as to what was motivating the man. He was not the generic womanizing man looking for the prettiest thing in a skirt, but rather the conquest of darkness over light. Perhaps inspired of the devil, he did not look for a spirit of compromise or sinfulness in others. He looked to bring sorrow and ruin to those who were committed to purity. Therefore, Tom felt attracted to godly women in that they presented to him the ultimate challenge.

❦❦❦❦

One morning as I was preparing the storefront, Tom came up to the register to make a phone call. He looked very sharp in a black turtleneck under a tweed jacket. I admired Tom's ability to dress very well on the small stipend we received at Harvest House. I knew he shopped at thrift stores and rumor had it that he even sewed clothes for himself. What an unusual man he was, I thought as he talked confidently on the phone, wheeling and dealing with one of his ministry connections.

"Did you hear what happened last night?" I heard Tom ask as I whirled around to see that he had hung up.

"No, what do you mean?" I wondered.

"We were trying to move the furniture into the mansion," Tom explained. "Michael was helping us, and he was tired and wanted to go home. It was taking too long for him, and he really lost it. He grabbed one of the chairs and almost threw it out of the van."

I was nervous. Tom had never gotten along with Michael, but they had so far succeeded in keeping their conflicts to themselves. Now Tom was criticizing my husband as if he wanted me to side with him against Michael. As he continued his complaint, he began to tell me how really valuable I was to "the work." His praise quickly rounded the bend and traveled down the road of flattery. A chill came over me as I realized what was going on, scarcely able to believe it. How could this *spiritual leader* actually be sowing these seeds of dissension between man and wife? How could this man who seemed so "led of God" be so *out of line*?

The day that followed was like something out of a sensational novel. Once Tom revealed his disrespect of my marriage, he was like a wild dog that had broken its chain. Again and again, Tom touched me unnecessarily and gave suggestive comments and looks. The fact that we were in the public eye kept me from reacting openly, but by the end of the day I was exasperated. Then Tom apologized.

But the spiritual tornado had just begun. Certain ones asked me about Tom's behavior. I admitted the truth. Tom found out. He became sullen and hateful toward me. I confronted him. He softened. But his softness turned into more familiarity. Eventually he made a direct pass at me. I feared his reaction if I told again, so I kept it all secret.

Then it got worse. I had refused his advances, telling myself that this would be enough to get him to leave me alone. I dreaded "telling," knowing that certain ones would blame me. After all, I reasoned, Tom was more "valuable" than I was to Harvest House. I would make a convenient scapegoat if push came to shove and it was my word against his. I loved being at Harvest House, and I didn't want to have to leave. I rationalized that I did not want to be a "tattletale," believing that I was strong enough to keep a level head without the support of others. But I came to realize that holding a secret for someone like Tom was a very risky business. It actually gave us something we shared that no one else knew. Not healthy.

One night, a fire was reported in the second restaurant, which was under construction. Three female workers, including myself, went with Tom to see what it was about. When we arrived, the restaurant was filled with smoke. The fire department came, but we had already found the problem, which was a burning coal, and doused it with water.

After the fire department left, Tom said that he needed to be dropped off at the airport right away. But someone needed to stay in the restaurant for a while to make sure the fire didn't have a second source somewhere. It sounded logical at the time, but now I realize Tom was scheming to be taken to the airport alone by one of us.

A girl named Katrina stayed while I and another young woman walked out with Tom. It was an understood policy that unmarried men and women were to avoid traveling alone together. But as we came to the street, Tom stopped in his tracks,

"You know, we can't leave her there alone," he said.

Now I was in a real dilemma. If I stayed, the other young woman would go alone with him. I didn't trust him with her. If she stayed, I would go alone with him, and I didn't trust him with me. But I felt I was stronger than my friend to resist him should he try something. Finally it was decided that I would go and the other two would wait for the van to pick them up.

Everything was fine until we came to a stoplight in front of the World Trade Towers, when Tom put his hand on mine and said, "You should never go anywhere alone with me."

That was pretty good advice considering how the rest of the trip went. When we finally arrived at the airport, he lunged at me. For the next several minutes, he persisted like a horsefly in spite of the fact that I swatted him away. It was almost comical. Finally, I slammed the car door in his face and tore out of Newark airport.

What Tom was doing in making the comment about being alone with him was trying to pass the blame on to me. The day after he made the first pass at me, he handed me a long letter telling me that it was all my fault. This was his effort to keep me from exposing him. It worked, for a while.

❦❦❦❦

The following morning was Sabbath. I was asked by a local church to provide a song during the worship service. I asked Linda Carlson to sing with me. The song we chose was one I wrote about the parable of the banquet feast. The chorus of the song invited people to respond to the gospel invitation:

Come, for all things are now ready
Come, a supper is prepared
Come, for you are one who is bidden
Come, there's so much to be shared.

The song went on to lament the many invitees who did not come. I was struck with the thought that being involved in a coverup was a form of lying. I knew that dishonesty could keep a person from that banqueting table in heaven. Conviction settled with a vice grip on my heart. I had to tell.

But who? I decided upon three people. Michael, who I knew I should have no secrets from, Linda, because she was Tom's wife and I needed to apologize for allowing the whole thing to go on so long, and David Grossman, who was more or less the spiritual leader of the group.

It was easy to tell David. In telling Michael I felt a little afraid, but immediate relief when he assured me that he did not think it was my fault. I can still remember his words, "You're a good girl, Jennifer." Not that I thought of myself as a "good girl," but I was glad he viewed me that way. It's always nice when your spouse believes in you.

Now, telling Linda Carlson was another story. She was a person who was naturally prone to judgmentalism. She helped maintain the high standards at the institution, but sometimes with a bit more acrimony than was necessary. Every time Tom would exhibit his immoral tendencies, the pressure on the women to dress and act "modestly" would increase. What was happening was that the women were being held responsible for what Tom was doing.

On top of her natural disposition to censure people, Linda was being pushed beyond her limits. Tom was acting out his love addiction with various ones in a more and more blatant way as she watched in agony and embarrassment. All of these complicated factors made telling Linda one of the hardest things I have ever had to do. *

My admission to her acted like a lance to a boil. The truth came spilling out—truth of other indiscretions with other women from years before. The domino effect set in. One thing led to another and soon several of his secrets were unearthed.

Monday, Tom called from Norway. Listening to his small voice over the receiver I perceived him as a beaten man. All the influence he once had over me was gone. *

❦ ❦ ❦ ❦

As soon as Tom returned, he discovered that I had confessed. I knew it was coming—the ill treatment, the malice, the cold war. For several weeks and even into months, Tom ignored me totally, which was difficult in that I was in a managerial position and needed to be able to communicate with him for practical reasons. I remember one morning sitting in a group and asking him something about a vehicle, and he acted as if he didn't hear or see me.

And it was tough emotionally—Tom was the "alpha male" of the

---

*Subsequent to leaving Harvest House, Tom filed for divorce. Since then Linda and I have discussed our experience at Harvest House in some depth. Much healing has taken place.

Writing this experience out has been a difficult undertaking. I feel a tension between the need to "Cry aloud, and spare not..." the sin of covert immorality and the call to "...considering thyself, lest thou also be tempted" (Isaiah 58:1 and Galatians 6:1, KJV). I feel my own weakness and inborn concupiscence to the core. I desire, and more importantly I know God desires, Tom to be saved. But the fact is that one who indulges in secret sexual sin is a danger, not only to him or herself, but to others in the church. In a broader arena of the Christian mission to the world, they are a danger to the church's reputation and therefore God's reputation. We are told not to let such things "...even be named among you..." and that we should "...Remove the wicked man from among yourselves" (Ephesians. 5:3, NKJ and 1 Corinthians 5:13, NAS). While the church needs to be a safe place for repentant sinners, we can't make it a safe place for sexual predators to practice their arts. May God help us all find the balance between justice and mercy when dealing with this issue.

herd, and being out of his good graces was not a pleasant experience. What I really desired from Tom was respect. But the "modus operandi" of a womanizer, be it conscious or not, is to withhold respect in order to create a sense of deprivation, and then offer familiarity in its place. There were two flip sides to Tom's behavior; an unnatural, cold reserve and a soft sentimentality. What was missing was the ability to be a Christian brother, supportive but dignified at the same time.

Eventually the edge wore off his harsh treatment of me. He would occasionally speak to me and at least acknowledge my presence. One day, Linda came to me with a question, "Tom wants to know if you are willing to work with him in the new restaurant. He feels that you are one of the best choices of people to be up front with the customers. Will you go?"

I was at that time running the health food store in the old restaurant while the crew worked on preparing the new restaurant in midtown Manhattan. Now the restaurant was ready to open.

"Ah . . . I'll have to think about it," I said dubiously. "I'll get back to you." I knew Linda was in a tough position, probably not wanting me to work with Tom, but wanting to cooperate with and support him.

I knew that I couldn't work in close quarters with Tom again. But I would ask Michael and let him say "no," which is exactly what happened. I returned to Linda with my answer. As soon as Tom found out, the harsh treatment started all over again. Tom would have been an incredible psychiatrist. He knew people. But he abused his gift. He used his knowledge of where people's buttons were to push them and create misery. It was done so subtly that he could technically claim he hadn't wronged the individual, but anyone who had been on his bad side knew how he could quietly make you suffer.

This time around I got a little bolder and determined to call the president of the board of the corporation that ran Harvest House. I knew that what was going on was totally wrong, and that Tom was unfit for the position he held. The only people that could do anything about that were the voting body of the board, the majority of which lived in other parts of the country. I reasoned that they needed correct information, not being physically present at the institution to witness what was going on. Naively, I spilled my story out to Dr. Franke, the president, one day on the phone.

"What Tom is doing is wrong! Because I refuse to work with him again, he is treating me like scum! Instead of respecting me and admitting that I'm right, he is treating me as if *I* am the criminal!"

But I realized shortly that Dr. Franke was in sympathy with Tom. "Well, we don't need to be condemning people," he said, "and don't you ever make mistakes?"

My mouth dropped as Dr. Franke continued. I couldn't believe what I was hearing. As far as Dr. Franke was concerned, what Tom was doing was no big deal. At least that's the way it seemed. Or maybe he didn't believe me . . . but that was hard to believe because he knew about several similar situations in which Tom was guilty of the same type of thing.

If it would have happened today, he may have taken it more seriously. Public awareness and legal options for dealing with sexual politics in the workplace have increased the chances of such situations being acted upon. And we have new terminology for such things. If only I had known what I know now, I would have said, "Dr. Franke, this is sexual harassment."

❦ ❦ ❦ ❦

The Harvest House crew was visiting a beautiful restaurant. The walls were covered with gorgeous paintings and there were several fancy shops on the premises. Women dressed in swanky outfits brought trays of food to the various people. It was a scene of splendor and enjoyment.

Suddenly, Linda Carlson's voice was heard, announcing the fact that the van would come soon, and that the crew should prepare to leave. With some disappointment we received this news, but we remained transfixed by the mesmerizing paintings.

"Aren't these beautiful?" I said, spotting David Grossman standing with his hands in his pockets. He was half looking at the paintings, but he seemed to be glancing around suspiciously at the same time, as if not convinced the place was safe.

"I don't really like them," he said, shaking his head, "or this place."

"David, are you crazy? This place is so incredible!" I said, taking in the marble floors and chandeliers.

"I just don't like it," he said with his usual skepticism.

I wandered away from David, still enjoying the surroundings, but wondering why he felt uncomfortable. David was a bit of a spiritual watchdog and I usually trusted his perceptions.

Suddenly I was informed that the proprietor of the establishment was requesting my presence on the top floor. Up the escalator I went, stepping into a high-ceilinged room with several of the women carrying trays gliding by. What was on those trays?

The manager was standing in the midst of several other important-looking men. He was dressed impeccably and had a confident air about him. His eyes rested upon me from across the room. Feeling suddenly like a country bumpkin in a royal palace, I froze while he approached me.

"Jennifer, we need you in this place. You have talents and abilities that could be developed with the right . . . training," he said, looking at my long flowered dress and clunky leather boots.

I blushed, comparing myself with the dainty women carrying those trays. What was on those trays? "Oh, well, I don't know about that," I demurred, not feeling special at all.

The man continued his pitch, seeming to drive toward asking me for a commitment. I felt the strange spirit of flattery in the air as he continued to use words like "exceptional" and "special" to describe me.

"You think about it," the man finally said with a wink, "I know you will make the right decision." With that he rejoined his cohorts and continued his business. I stood watching as he walked away. I thought about his offer. I wanted to be part of it all, but something held me back from trusting.

Returning to the ground floor, I saw the crew still staring at the paintings.

"Is the van coming?" I said, now anxious to leave.

"Yeah," a voice sighed, "it should be here soon."

But several minutes later, nothing had changed.

The conviction seized me that I could not wait for the van to come. I had to find a way to get out myself, for I could depend upon no one, not Linda Carlson, not David Grossman, *no one* to get me out. I had a sense that I was totally without human support.

Running to a pay phone, I dialed my mother to ask her for a ride. As the phone rang, I turned to look once more on the place, the gorgeous paintings, the rich decor, and those fancy women with trays. What was on those trays?

Like a lightening flash out of nowhere the realization hit me. The trays contained human flesh. The restaurant was in the business of serving *human flesh!*

Gasping for breath and sitting upright in my bed, I woke.

❦❦❦❦

<u>*Chance of Rain*</u>

The sky is bright without a cloud
The thirsting people cry out loud
The sun and wind will parch the grain
And still there is a chance of rain

We've talked of how our river flows
But where's the verdure? No one knows
We boast that we have crop to spare
While desert winds blow through out hair

It's not a force that lays us flat
It's not a tug of war
It's not as if God held it back
In archive days of yore
It's not a thing we bring to pass
With vigils on our knees
It's a gift, it always was
We would not receive

Our hearts are hard as bone-dry ground
Not even tears have trickled down
We beg for what you freely share
And then refuse it with a prayer

It's not a wrestling match with God
It's not a weight we lift
It's not our place to sweat the blood
That bought the precious gift
It's ground so dry it finally cracks
It's hearts that finally break
It's a gift, God can't hold back
We can't seem to take

From the CD *Chance of Rain.*

❦❦❦❦

CHAPTER 21

Travail

Winter, 1986.

A powerful angel hovers over a woman lying on a hospital bed in the OB wing of Stoneycreek Hospital in Tennessee. Several nurses surround her as she moans as if dying, rocking back and forth. A nurse tries to hold a metal contraption to her swollen belly.

"Get that thing off of me," the moaning woman says under her breath.

"She seems irritable," chimes one of the nurses, "she doesn't want that fetal monitor on her. I think she's in transition."

"You are about to meet your new charge," said the powerful angel in an undetected voice. Beside the angel hovered a fresh-faced smaller angel.

"I'm ready," said the fresh-faced angel, "I wonder if it will be male or female."

"She's fully dilated and I can't find the cervix," one of the nurses said wistfully. A shocked-looking head nurse ran out the door, returning with Jillian Johnson, the OB doctor.

"So I hear you wanna have a baby!" Jillian shouted with a laugh in her voice.

"Yes, I do, right now," the woman moaned, "tell them to leave me alone and let me have my baby."

"What's the cervix doing?" Jillian asked the head nurse.

"She's ready," the nurse nodded nervously.

"Ready?" even Jillian seemed a little shocked, "Well, let's go then!"

she said, recovering herself and shouting as she scanned the circle of faces. This labor had been short for a prima gravida, she thought.

Suddenly the room broke into a frenzy. A dark-haired, bearded man ran into the bathroom and, leaning out of the door while he put on a blue scrub jacket and pants, shouted, "Wait, Jen! I'm coming!"

"We're bringing her into delivery!" Jillian called.

The patient shook off the nurses arms and walked to the delivery table, and lay down with her feet where her head should have been.

"Let her go through this contraction, then turn her around," said Jillian above the moaning of the laboring woman and the clatter of medical paraphernalia. When the moaning subsided, the woman swung herself around.

"Now PUSH!" shouted Jillian, walking to the foot of the table, looking up at the patient.

Only a few minutes and agonizing contractions later, the baby was out and wailing away.

The powerful angel put a strong arm on the shoulder of the fresh-faced angel. "Welcome your new human friend," he said as the baby was handed to her father.

"This is your Father's beard!" the elated father sang as the wailing newborn seemed to reach out and touch the man's black beard.

Jillian laughed. "This kid doesn't stand a chance," she said, only to stop smiling totally when she saw a river of blood.

❦ ❦ ❦ ❦

There are certain points in life when you reevaluate your belief system. Those points are usually triggered by a crisis or problem that awakens you to the fact that, old methods and attitudes are insufficient to handle the growing complexities in your path. In short, there are turning points when old ways of thinking become obsolete. I was now in the midst of such a time.

Since my days at Woodhollow, I had approached the Seventh-day Adventist religion with black-and-white glasses on. I accepted the doctrines. I believed in the prophet. I followed the counsels to the letter. All was well until I realized that, although I was outwardly righteous, I was vulnerable to deception. Why hadn't the program worked? I did not have the answer, but I had a desire to find it.

And God was preparing me to receive the answer, but first He had to break up the fallow ground of my heart in preparation for the seed of truth. What better way to do this than to allow me to accidentally become pregnant?

I was not anxious to have children, but I did not want to completely block the way to motherhood in case God willed it. So I compromised by using a method of birth control that had about a 3% failure rate. "If God wants to make the nearly impossible happen, He can!" I thought, not really believing it would. I had so much I wanted to do, so many dreams and creative ideas. Children would slow me down and force me to stay holed up at home, I thought.

When the queasy feeling of morning sickness came, I assumed it was just an intestinal bug. But it lingered. Then came the home pregnancy test with positive results. Apparently, God did want me to become a mother. Duh.

I broke the news to Michael and gradually everyone else at the institution. Michael and I were told that we could move into a trailer when the baby was born, but there was no money or time to furnish a house for us. Michael and I had to evaluate our situation there. Living in a trailer did not bother him, but I couldn't envision it. And I was at Harvest House for the opportunities to work in New York City. Staying on the farm with the other mothers and staring at the walls of a trailer most of the day did not sound like a life to me.

And there were other drawbacks to staying. The rift between Michael and me and Tom was ever present, and apparently Tom was staying in the directorship position. Numerous board meetings had come and gone in which members had grappled with what was going on, and for some reason they came to the conclusion that they should leave him there. This was strange considering his immoral activities were not limited to the things that happened with me. But neither Michael nor I were on the board, so we had little influence to change the course of events.

Then one day Michael revealed his heart to me. "I have to leave, Jennifer. Even if you stay, I'm leaving," he said. So the writing was on the wall. There was no relationship on earth that was as sacred as marriage. Only my relationship to God Himself was more of a priority.

I reflected back upon the dream of the women serving human flesh. I believe the dream was God's way of telling me I needed to leave the Harvest House community. I couldn't depend upon friends to tell me my individual duty to God. It had become a danger for me to stay there. As much as my attachments there were deep, and as sad as I was about leaving, I knew it was time.

I felt the need to be up front with Tom about my decision. He seemed quite calm when I told him, but then he began to reason with me in a way that sounded very much like the thoughts the man had expressed in the dream. "You need to think about something, Jennifer," he said, "If you leave here, your talents will never be used. I have seen you grow so much these last five years, and I hate to see you go back to a situation where you will be cut off from people."

Tom knew enough about the rough spots in my marriage to paint it in its darkest dye. There was some truth to what he said—Mike was more reserved than I and some of the situations he had chosen for us were too isolated for me. But Tom inferred that it would always be that way. It was true that Michael and I had unresolved difficulties in our marriage, but Tom insinuated that we could *never* resolve them. Gloom and doom poured out of Tom as he tried to convince me that staying at Harvest House was the only way I could be fulfilled. "Jennifer, read *Christ's Object Lessons,* page 224 through 225," he said, finally, "you'll see what I mean."

I went home and opened my little paperback copy of the book. The passage was a commentary on Luke 14:16-24, which is the parable of the call to the banquet. Several people were called to a dinner party that represented heaven. They all gave excuses, including one who said, "I have married a wife" (v. 20, NKJ). The passage from Ellen G. White's *Christ's Object Lessons* comments on this, warning against "refuse [ing] the Saviour's call because they fear division in the family circle."

Tom's implication was that I was refusing the Savior's call to stay at the institute because of my familial attachment to my husband. I could see that this was a gross distortion of the message of that passage. Tom was saying that in leaving the institution, Michael was leaving God. It followed that, if I left with Michael, I would be putting him before God and "refuse [ing] the Saviour's call."

This didn't actually surprise me. Tom was trying to use guilt to control me, which was all part of his obsession with power. Tom had lost true spiritual power because his connection with God was broken. Sensing his loss of power, he resorted to using coercive power, and carried out what amounted to a spiritual inquisition. But thank God, I was totally fortified against his ploy at this point. I called him on the phone.

"Tom, I just want you to know that I read the passage you asked me to read. What you are trying to say is that I would be walking away from God by leaving with my husband. Well, you are wrong. My commitment to Michael is more sacred than my commitment to this place," I said, expecting him to argue back.

Tom didn't disappoint my expectations. His tone grew aggressive, "You are throwing your life away! Don't you know that you will never do what you could do if you stayed here? Don't be stupid."

"I can't ignore my conscience!" I countered.

"No, but you can sear it!" he spit the words out like nails into a coffin, and after a click, the phone went dead.*

❦ ❦ ❦ ❦

For months and even years after we left Harvest House, I mourned the loss of what was and what could have been. A beautiful farm, a thriving restaurant business, a topnotch team of people, it all had the makings of a fantastic ministry. And it was. But the destruction that Satan could not bring about through external pressure and hardship he accomplished through internal compromise. Like the Christian

---

*My desire in relating these events is not to sensationalize what occurred. I relate the downfalls of individuals only as they intersect with my story. As for the one I have named Tom Carlson, the door of mercy is still open for you. "He who conceals his transgressions will not prosper, But he who confesses and forsakes them will find compassion" (Proverbs 28:13, NAS).

As for the network of institutions that I was a part of, and still exists, I do not wish to cast aspersions upon a branch of God's work which I perceive as doing good in this world. I learned much of value during my years at Woodhollow and Harvest House, and still practice those valuable things. I took more good than bad away. But in order to rightly represent my own spiritual journey, I must share the truth of what I experienced.

church that was invincible during persecution, Harvest House was an irrepressible force for good in godless New York City. But like the church, there was eventual *internal* compromise that led to self-destruction. One by one the team members left as Michael and I did, unable to work with Tom.

How might this disintegration have been prevented? I would be stupid not to ask that hard question. I have come to realize there was one major flaw in our method and spirit that proved to be the Achille's heel of the organization. In a nutshell, we were separatists.

Although we did not express it openly, there was a feeling among the crew of Harvest House that we were superior to others in the church. The reason for this was that we "followed the counsels" of Ellen White—we thought—much more faithfully than those who comprised the mainstream Adventist Church. Our diet and our dress was, on the surface, in more perfect harmony with what she advised. We were in restaurant ministry, which was also in obedience to counsel. While these things were good in and of themselves, our spirit and attitude was at times far from right. Subtly, quietly, we cherished feelings of superiority to our brothers and sisters, and instead of seeing ourselves as part of a whole, we maintained the idea that we were complete within ourselves.

Instead of worshipping at a local Seventh-day Adventist church, we had our own "home church" on the farm. There were no local pastors or other leaders on the Harvest House board. When any group becomes insular and isolated as we did, the danger of corruption increases manifold. I see now that if we had more accountability and involvement with the mainstream church, it may have prevented some of the devastation.

But a deeper problem lay at the root of our separatism. Like many conservatives, our great downfall was pride. The liberal camp of the church may fall down in the area of standards, but the conservative camp has its own specious sin, that of Pharisaism. We cherished a subtle spirit of "holier than thou" until we were a fulfillment of the proverb, "pride goeth before a fall."

❦ ❦ ❦ ❦

As a stepping stone from Harvest House to the "real world," Michael and I moved to another community in the south where I was to give birth to our first child. The community had a small hospital that I worked in while I awaited the delivery. Michael worked locally planting trees.

I was a bit worried about what kind of mother I would be. My natural desire was to inhabit the adult world. I observed friends with children and wondered how I would ever find the patience to deal with constant interruption, runny noses and dirty diapers. Until the day my child was born, I feared that I would be a cold, indifferent mother.

When I was two weeks overdue, the doctor decided to break my water, which prompted labor. I opted for natural, drug-free childbirth, and used breathing exercises to help deal with the painful contractions. Michael was there, my only link to sanity through the most intense pain I had ever felt. Five hours later I gave birth to a beautiful baby girl, and then proceeded to hemorrhage dreadfully. Medical people were flying around frantically while Michael and I laughed and cried over our newborn child. I thank God for modern medicine and good medical care in that I may not have lived to raise my child without them.

Once I was settled into my hospital room for the night, I placed my tiny infant next to me. My body still ached and trembled from the ordeal of birth, but in contrast the baby was so whole, so perfect, and so peaceful. Suddenly, the affection that I feared I could never have for an infant hit me like a tidal wave. I felt my heart come out of itself and reach for this little soul that was so totally dependent upon me. This child's happiness, her health, her salvation, her entire future, was largely held in my hands. Awed and yet graced by the calling of motherhood, I found myself praying as I looked upon her tiny form.

Suddenly the Lord seemed to be giving me a revelation of Himself. I remembered that Jesus called His people "...the travail of His soul..." (Isaiah 53:11, KJV). "Travail" was a biblical word that was sometimes used to describe the process of labor (see Isaiah 42:14). God seemed to be telling me that labor was a metaphor of Christ's death on the cross. My body was broken while bringing forth my child's wholeness. There she lay, oblivious to the pain that was required to bring her forth to life. How like sleepy Laodicea, I thought, unaware of the ongoing hurt our infantile sin was bringing to the heart of Christ. "Is it nothing to you, all ye that pass by?" He asks, "behold, and see if there be any sorrow like unto my sorrow…" (Lamentations 1:12, KJV). There I held her, feeling nothing but love for her that had torn me in two. How like Christ, I thought, who holds not a drop of resentment in His suffering love for us. Because of these thoughts God had laid upon my heart, childbirth for me was like a second conversion. I felt I had been brought face to face with the suffering love of God.

❦ ❦ ❦ ❦

Michael and I, along with our newborn baby, were on our own in the world for the first time in six years. I knew that we would probably not go back to a place like Harvest House or Woodhollow. It was time for us to find our place in the mainstream Seventh-day Adventist Church. This was difficult because neither Michael nor I had family in the church. Most of our friends were in the institutions we had spent so much time in. In so many ways, we were starting from scratch.

The canvas was wiped clean. Upon it have come the brushstrokes of the last thirteen years. Most of the events of those years are for another time, another book. But there is one more important passage in my journey that I must relate. God had yet one more golden link in the chain of truth to reveal to Michael and me. Shortly after we left Harvest House, we discovered the most precious message of righteousness by faith.

CHAPTER 22

Most Precious Message

Spring, 1986.

A man stood before a small crowd that had gathered inside a red brick church in Leominster, Massachusetts. It was about 7:00 P.M. on Saturday. "I'm sorry we are so few in number," he said, "but the Lord is here, and the angels are too."

Behind an unseen veil a retinue of bright, holy angels said, "Amen!"

After the man offered prayer, a young woman handed a small baby over to a gray-haired lady in the front pew, then stood and strapped on a guitar. As she began to play, her soprano voice floated up to the ceiling to the hum of guitar strings. The angels sang along in an undetected harmony, which floated up to heaven like a cloud of incense.

Several dark, ugly angels crouched in the back pews. A few got up and walked out in disgust. The ones who remained seemed pained to hear the simple testimony in song pouring out of the young woman.

"Oh, this hurts," said a dark angel with a twisted face, "we have to stop this somehow!"

"I thought she would be silenced by discouragement, and now it's even worse!" said an angel with strangely slanted eyes, "She's happier than she's ever been. What now?"

The dark, ugly angel seemed conflicted. "Well, the logical thing to do would be to kill that voice!" he said, shrugging his wart-covered shoulders.

The other angel looked blankly at him and said, "You'd have to get permission, you know, and I know how you hate to do that."

The ugly angel with a twisted face thought for a moment, then replied, "I do. I hate to ask permission. But that voice will do nothing but warble about the One I hate so much . . . so I think we need to kill the voice."

❦ ❦ ❦ ❦

The transition time between living at Harvest House and the "real world" was a tough one for me. It takes a while to find your niche, and I didn't really have one right away. We moved to Connecticut and lived with another family for a year while we were getting on our feet. Most of the time was spent enjoying my baby's development and my husband's company. This was good in a way because we needed the time to bond as a family. But once the bonding was done, I was bored.

Thankfully, a new development took place. Friends began to ask me to sing for their churches, not just one song during the church service, but whole concerts. This gave me a chance to share the scores of songs I was writing. One thing led to another, and pretty soon I was doing a concert most every weekend. This was the beginning of a ministry that has lasted thirteen years and counting. And yes, I have lost my voice, more than once. But that story is for another time.

❦ ❦ ❦ ❦

One weekend Mike and I decided to visit some old friends from Harvest House. The Flower's were actually from as far back as Woodhollow days. Dalton Flowers ran a wholesale health-food business and his wife, Daisy (making her full name Daisy Flowers) was a mother of three. They had a new baby as well, a little boy with puffy white hair that made him into a human dandelion.

Dalton, whose nickname was "Bud" (making him Bud Flowers) was a talented businessman who had lifted several ministries out of debt through his wholesale health-food businesses. He was a busy man—he would work such long hours that at times he would get fungal infections in his ears from being on the phone so much. Harvest House had been rough on him in that his relationship with Tom Carlson became impossible. The Flower's left shortly before we did, and just like us they struggled to process their experience.

But observing Bud now was like meeting a new person. His melancholy temperament was offset by a certain joy I had never noticed in him before. He seemed energized, even elated. As we walked, he talked to Michael, and I eavesdropped.

"And this book I've been reading tells all about what happened in 1888. From what I've learned, it was a very important time for the church. These two preachers, Jones and Waggoner, shared a message that Ellen White affirmed hundreds of times. She said in response to hearing it, 'Every fiber of my heart said "Amen!" ' " *(The Ellen G. White 1888 Materials*, 348, paragraph 4).

I didn't think much about what Bud said except that I noted how happy "1888" had made him. I wasn't anxious to get involved in some strenuous ideology, but it seemed to help him. Good, I thought, whatever floats your boat.

A few weeks later, Bud invited us to a large church in New York where a certain speaker would come to talk about the 1888 message. At his encouragement, we went. We were amazed at the packed church and the level of excitement we felt there.

The speaker was a white-haired fellow who talked while flying through numerous overheads of long Ellen White quotations. His burden was to establish the fact that the message given by Jones and Waggoner was the "most precious message" of Christ's righteousness and the "third angel's message in verity." The world would be "lightened with His glory," when it was preached by a united church, he claimed. (*The Ellen G. White 1888 Materials*, 1336, paragraph 2; *The Review and Herald*, April 1, 1890; Revelation 18:1). He told of the fact that, when the message came in 1888, many of the established leaders of the church felt no need of it, and so it was not fully embraced or proclaimed. He read several statements that indicated that Jesus would have come if it had been (*G.C. Bulletin*, 1893, P. 419; *Review and Herald* Dec. 24, 1903).

Wow, I thought, this is heavy. The delay of Jesus' coming was a serious thing. The evidence was strong, but I was wary. I was hearing a whole new language and emphasis. I wondered if the followers of the 1888 message were their own little society within the church, and I was not anxious to join another special-interest group. Even though Bud Flowers and David Grossman were enthusiastic about it, I had learned not to follow others' ideas without studying for myself. But being a seeker for truth I felt that I needed to at least examine the evidence before I rejected the idea. Michael felt the same way I did—curious but cautious—and so we determined to research the issue on our own. We bought several books and went home to read.

❦ ❦ ❦ ❦

Bob Conklin was an evangelist of no small talents. A tall, congenial fellow with twinkly blue eyes, he made friends wherever he went. At one point God had impressed him to come to Harvest House and learn about restaurant work in hopes of eventually being able to plant a Harvest House Restaurant in the Boston area where he lived and worked. When we finally settled in Eastern Connecticut, Bob had a large influence upon Michael and me, and my sister Kristin as well, who eventually accepted a job from him as a Bible worker. We heard him preach at a convention in New Hampshire, and afterwards cornered him with questions.

"Is this 1888 message just another fad, or is it something we should really pay attention to?" I asked, trying to rock my baby to sleep and talk at the same time.

"Well, I have to admit that my heart has been strangely warmed by it," he said, smiling alternately at Michael and me. Bob was not willing to push his beliefs, so his answers were subtle.

"I read about it years ago," said Michael, "and I always thought it was something we should study."

"But how are we supposed to know if all this stuff is true," I implored, "when they get their statements out of the Ellen White archives? I don't have time to do all this research, but I don't want to just take their word for it."

Bob chuckled, "Well, I don't think you should have to worry about that. Your main concern is in your lap," he said, looking down upon my wiggling baby. "But the prophet said that 'many had lost sight of Jesus' in 1888, and that same thing is true of us today. We need our eyes to be refocused upon Christ. And the 1888 message has done that for me' " (*The Ellen G. White 1888 Materials,* 1336, paragraph 2).

I had to agree with him. Somehow in the midst of Adventism I had let other issues loom larger than the One whose advent I awaited.

❦ ❦ ❦ ❦

Several books and sermons later, I became convinced that there was something to it all. As I sat at future conferences and meetings, my heart was moved by the simple beauty of what was shared. As my mind was opened up to this truth, several things became clear to me.

For the first time in my Christian experience I could understand what was meant by "righteousness by faith." I had heard the terminology before, and even been engaged in bouts of discussion at different junctures of my journey, but never had I felt confident that I understood the relationship of faith and obedience.

Now I realized that I had unconsciously hoped that adherence to the counsel of Ellen White would better my status with God. I learned that if I was to be saved by obedience, I was "...under obligation to keep the whole Law" (Galatians 5:3, NAS). And the Bible was clear that "...all have sinned and fall short of the glory of God" (Romans 3:23, NAS), so keeping the whole law was impossible for me. Thankfully, I learned, God had another plan. It was called the "New Covenant," and its terms were, not obey and live, but *believe and live* (*Patriarchs and Prophets,* 372). Through faith in His merits, I could access the saving grace of God. Then my life would be transformed from the inside out and obedience would follow. My works would be a fruit of salvation and not a means of it.

Another product of this revelation was a reassessment of what a true Christian would look like. I had accustomed myself to making judgments of Adventists based upon how they dressed and what they ate. If they, like me, were reformers, I felt more favorable toward them. If they were more liberal in their lifestyle, or what I would call "Laodicean," I would unconsciously judge them as either backslidden or ignorant.

All of this was greatly challenged when some of my reformer friends showed their true colors. Tom Carlson, for instance, felt that short sleeves were immodest and unhealthful. I had received a lecture from him when I wore elbow-length sleeves in 90 degree weather instead of long sleeves. Yet he was willing to secretly break the seventh commandment. The words of Jesus came to mind, "Woe unto you . . . which strain at a gnat and swallow a camel" (Matthew 23:23,24, KJV). Had we, as the passage also said, "...neglected the weightier provisions of the law..." (v. 23, NAS)? I had to admit it was so.

As a result of this realization I formed a new concept of what constituted a true Christian. Rather than focusing on the "gnats," a Christian would reflect the character of Jesus in their manner of relating to their fellow man. In other words, true obedience would lead a person to love other people unselfishly, with God-given *agape* love. Reforms would be carried out in the spirit of this love. Agape and all that it entailed was what Jesus referred to as the "weightier provisions of the law."

I had adopted the reforms with a motive of "this is good for me." Now God was moving my focus until it was others-directed instead of self-directed. It was as if I had been given a new pair of glasses. I saw the lifestyle issues in the light of God's love.

Another tool I was given was the ability to be part of the mainstream of the church God had led me to. I had always felt somehow separate from what I perceived to be sleepy Laodicea. Now I realized that I *was* part of Laodicea, whether I was in a special group or not. God did not qualify His statement to that church in Revelation 3:16-18 by saying, "certain ones of you are lukewarm" or "all of you are lukewarm except the reformers." He addressed the church as a whole. I realized through this that the sins of the church were my sins in the collective sense. No longer could I deceive myself into thinking that I was somehow set apart and special. Like Daniel, I learned to pray, "*we* have sinned . . ." (Daniel 9:5, NAS).

And out of this ability to identify with the sins of God's church came the ability to love the members of that same church. It is true that realizing the depth of our own depravity can short-circuit our ability to love others. On the flip side of that is the fact that our failure to love one another stems from our denial. "...he who is forgiven little, loves little" (Luke 7:47, NAS).

Now when I read from the Bible, truth had a cohesiveness it had never had before. Since I had first become a Seventh-day Adventist, I had studied the Bible every day, but to some extent it was because I knew I should. Now I was motivated to deep study because I had a pair of glasses through which every truth of the Bible, including distinctive Adventist doctrines, was resplendent with the beauty of Jesus. My heart was warmed with a new vision of the "matchless charms of Christ" (*The Ellen G. White 1888 Materials,* 348, paragraph 4).

My Christian experience has been an ongoing process of weaning away from the legalism that is inborn and inbred. Once I believed that meditating and fasting would earn enlightenment. Then once I became a Christian, I unconsciously believed that my good works would save me. Time and time again God brings me back to the same reality; it's not my job to save myself, it's God's job. My job is to let Him do what He is best at.

> The sinner may resist this love, may refuse to be drawn to Christ; but if he does not resist he will be drawn to Jesus; a knowledge of the plan of salvation will lead him to the foot of the cross in repentance for his sins, which have caused the sufferings of God's dear Son (*Steps to Christ*, 27).

❦❦❦❦

Many years have come and gone. Michael and I have continued our search for truth, and we are more fulfilled and happier than we have ever been. Over the last decade, we have been able to form a network of friends that spans the world. My music ministry has taken me all over the country and to Europe, Africa and Canada, and I have continued to write and record the songs God gives me.

Most weekends for the last thirteen years I have appeared in a church, coffeehouse, or other venue to sing or preach. I have developed two seminars that I have shared in numerous churches, schools and camp meetings. In this sense I have continued to be a "lay ministry." But I am able to see myself as a part of the whole of the church, rather than part of an elite group. I have come to enjoy the unity within diversity that is found in the family of God.

Michael and I have been able to strike a compromise that suits both of our temperaments. My need for public life is met through music and seminar ministry, but Michael's need for space is met by living on our own. I have come to appreciate the quiet. For one thing, I have been able to use the time to develop my talents. For another thing, a quieter life has been a wonderful environment in which to raise children. We have not one, but two beautiful daughters, for Kimberly was born two years after Alison.

My search for truth will never end. I thank God for the unfolding revelation of Himself to me. First He led me out of New Age into a knowledge of Jesus Christ. Reaching out from the foundation of biblical Christianity, I was led to the Seventh-day Adventist message. Within the gold mine of knowledge bequeathed to this church, I discovered the most precious message of righteousness by faith. And there is more to come . . .

Now my two girls are coasting into adolescence, the point in my experience at which I began this book. As I watch them blossom into young women, I relive my own teenage years. Pray for them. They, like each one of us, are citadels of God-given free will. Life stretches out before them like a tightrope over a roaring river. I remember a time when it seemed that I would fall into the torrent, never to be retrieved. But I stand on solid ground today because Jesus did not count heaven a place to be desired while I was lost.

I never thought I would live to see my children grow up. The coming of Jesus seemed to be only months away when I first embraced the truth of the Second Advent. As tragic as the delay is, there is one positive element. You and I have an opportunity to be, not only seekers, but vessels of the truth that will one day lighten the earth with His glory. Let not one of us refuse that call.

Other products by Jennifer Jill Schwirzer:

Chance of Rain

Jennifer Jill. Songs of Christ's passion to save and fill us. Songs include "Gethsemane Angel," "Anathema; The God-Forsaken God," "Were You There?" "In Christ Medley," "Chance of Rain," and others. CD:4-3330-0218-4; C: 4-3330-0218-5. US$15.98, Cdn$23.99.

Gospel Moments

Jennifer Jill. Stories, songs and scriptures that teach children about salvation. Five cassettes, US$6.98, Cdn$10.49 each, or US$29.98, Cdn$44.99 for entire 5 volume set.

Vol. 1: God's Love and Christ's Humanity. C:4-3330-0074-6.

Vol. 2: The Sanctuary and Joy in Trials. C:4-3330-0074-8.

Vol. 3: The Power of Faith and Beholding Christ. C:4-3330-0074-9.

Vol. 4: Mary Magdalene and the Motive of Love. C:4-3330-0075-0.

Vol. 5: Christ's Coming, Heaven and the New Covenant: C:4-3330-0075-1.

5 Vol. Set: C:4-3330-0075-2.

If you enjoyed this book, you'll enjoy these as well:

Be My Angel

Harriet Canne. As Meredith searches for answers about life, death, and what comes after, she discovers that things aren't always as they appear. It isn't until a terrifying encounter with a Ouija board that she realizes she's been lured into the dark world of the occult by a rather innocent-looking deck of angel cards. A story of the search for truth and the subtle deceptions of Satan. 0-8163-1708-9. Paperback. US$11.99, Cdn$17.49.

Dark Refuge

Andy Demsky. A chilling story that exposes the destructive path that leads many into religious cults. Discover how Anita was nearly seduced into surrendering her life, and how she escaped to find the God who always loved her.0-8163-1241-9. US$11.99, Cdn$17.49.

Falling For A Lie

Jay Christian as told to *Helen Heavirland.* Jay Christian grew up searching for truth. What he found was New Age deceptions. His story dramatically shows how seemingly innocent New Age practices lead to deeper involvement, and points out how Bible truths refute the New Age teachings of reincarnation, karma, and psychics. 0-8163-1646-5. Paperback. US$10.99, Cdn$15.99.

Journal of a Not-So-Perfect Daughter

Nancy Carver Abbott. An intensely honest look into the heart of a woman struggling in her relationship with her father and her relationship with God. 0-8163-1650-3. Paperback. US$10.99, Cdn$15.99.

Order from your ABC by calling **1-800-765-6955**, or get online and shop our virtual store at **www.adventistbookcenter.com**.

Read a chapter from your favorite book

Order online

Sign up for e-mail notices on new products